Juvenile Crime

OPPOSING VIEWPOINTS®

D0067494

Juvenile Crime

OPPOSING VIEWPOINTS®

Other Books of Related Interest

Juvenile Crime

OPPOSING VIEWPOINTS®

Auriana Ojeda, *Book Editor*

Daniel Leone, *Publisher*

Bonnie Szumski, *Editorial Director*

Scott Barbour, *Managing Editor*

OPPOSING
VIEWPOINTS®
SERIES

Greenhaven Press, Inc., San Diego, California

Cover photo: Photodisc

Library of Congress Cataloging-in-Publication Data

Juvenile crime : opposing viewpoints / Auriana Ojeda, book editor.
    p.   cm. — (Opposing viewpoints series)
    Includes bibliographical references and index.
    ISBN 0-7377-0783-6 (pbk. : alk. paper) —
ISBN 0-7377-0784-4 (lib. : alk. paper)
    1. Juvenile delinquency. I. Ojeda, Auriana, 1977–
II. Opposing viewpoints series (Unnumbered)

HV9069 .J78 2002
364.36—dc21   2001023310
                                                          CIP

Greenhaven Press, Inc., P.O. Box 289009
San Diego, CA 92198-9009

"Congress shall make no law. . . abridging the freedom of speech, or of the press."

First Amendment to the U.S. Constitution

The basic foundation of our democracy is the First Amendment guarantee of freedom of expression. The Opposing Viewpoints Series is dedicated to the concept of this basic freedom and the idea that it is more important to practice it than to enshrine it.

Contents

Chapter 3: What Factors Contribute to Gang-Related Juvenile Crime?

Chapter 4: How Can Juvenile Crime and Violence Be Combated?

Why Consider Opposing Viewpoints?

"The only way in which a human being can make some approach to knowing the whole of a subject is by hearing what can be said about it by persons of every variety of opinion and studying all modes in which it can be looked at by every character of mind. No wise man ever acquired his wisdom in any mode but this."

John Stuart Mill

In our media-intensive culture it is not difficult to find differing opinions. Thousands of newspapers and magazines and dozens of radio and television talk shows resound with differing points of view. The difficulty lies in deciding which opinion to agree with and which "experts" seem the most credible. The more inundated we become with differing opinions and claims, the more essential it is to hone critical reading and thinking skills to evaluate these ideas. Opposing Viewpoints books address this problem directly by presenting stimulating debates that can be used to enhance and teach these skills. The varied opinions contained in each book examine many different aspects of a single issue. While examining these conveniently edited opposing views, readers can develop critical thinking skills such as the ability to compare and contrast authors' credibility, facts, argumentation styles, use of persuasive techniques, and other stylistic tools. In short, the Opposing Viewpoints Series is an ideal way to attain the higher-level thinking and reading skills so essential in a culture of diverse and contradictory opinions.

In addition to providing a tool for critical thinking, Opposing Viewpoints books challenge readers to question their own strongly held opinions and assumptions. Most people form their opinions on the basis of upbringing, peer pressure, and personal, cultural, or professional bias. By reading carefully balanced opposing views, readers must directly confront new ideas as well as the opinions of those with whom they disagree. This is not to simplistically argue that everyone who reads opposing views will—or should—change his or her opinion. Instead, the series enhances readers' understanding of their own views by encouraging confrontation with opposing ideas. Careful examination of others' views can lead to the readers' understanding of the logical inconsistencies in their own opinions, perspective on why they hold an opinion, and the consideration of the possibility that their opinion requires further evaluation.

Evaluating Other Opinions

To ensure that this type of examination occurs, Opposing Viewpoints books present all types of opinions. Prominent spokespeople on different sides of each issue as well as well-known professionals from many disciplines challenge the reader. An additional goal of the series is to provide a forum for other, less known, or even unpopular viewpoints. The opinion of an ordinary person who has had to make the decision to cut off life support from a terminally ill relative, for example, may be just as valuable and provide just as much insight as a medical ethicist's professional opinion. The editors have two additional purposes in including these less known views. One, the editors encourage readers to respect others' opinions—even when not enhanced by professional credibility. It is only by reading or listening to and objectively evaluating others' ideas that one can determine whether they are worthy of consideration. Two, the inclusion of such viewpoints encourages the important critical thinking skill of objectively evaluating an author's credentials and bias. This evaluation will illuminate an author's reasons for taking a particular stance on an issue and will aid in readers' evaluation of the author's ideas.

It is our hope that these books will give readers a deeper understanding of the issues debated and an appreciation of the complexity of even seemingly simple issues when good and honest people disagree. This awareness is particularly important in a democratic society such as ours in which people enter into public debate to determine the common good. Those with whom one disagrees should not be regarded as enemies but rather as people whose views deserve careful examination and may shed light on one's own.

Thomas Jefferson once said that "difference of opinion leads to inquiry, and inquiry to truth." Jefferson, a broadly educated man, argued that "if a nation expects to be ignorant and free . . . it expects what never was and never will be." As individuals and as a nation, it is imperative that we consider the opinions of others and examine them with skill and discernment. The Opposing Viewpoints Series is intended to help readers achieve this goal.

David L. Bender and Bruno Leone,
Founders

Greenhaven Press anthologies primarily consist of previously published material taken from a variety of sources, including periodicals, books, scholarly journals, newspapers, government documents, and position papers from private and public organizations. These original sources are often edited for length and to ensure their accessibility for a young adult audience. The anthology editors also change the original titles of these works in order to clearly present the main thesis of each viewpoint and to explicitly indicate the opinion presented in the viewpoint. These alterations are made in consideration of both the reading and comprehension levels of a young adult audience. Every effort is made to ensure that Greenhaven Press accurately reflects the original intent of the authors included in this anthology.

Introduction

"Like television, our cinemas are full of movies that glamorize bloodshed and violence, and one need only listen to popular music radio . . . to see that our music . . . [is] similarly afflicted."

Orrin G. Hatch, U.S. Senator

"The scientific evidence does not support the view that exposure to media violence causes aggression."

Jonathan Freedman, psychology professor

In 1997, fourteen-year-old Michael Carneal fired a .22 caliber handgun at an informal prayer group in his high school in West Paducah, Kentucky, killing three students and wounding five. In 1998 in Pearl, Mississippi, sixteen-year-old Luke Woodham first killed his mother, and then went to school and shot nine students, killing two. In the same year, fifteen-year-old Kip Kinkel shot and killed his parents and two classmates and wounded twenty-three others. In 2000, a first-grader in Michigan shot and killed another six-year-old after a schoolyard quarrel the day before.

Events such as these have raised concerns about an increase in juvenile crime despite statistics that reveal a decline. According to the Justice Department, the juvenile arrest rate is at its lowest level since 1966, having decreased 68 percent from 1993 to 1999. The arrest rates for four major crimes—robbery, rape, murder, and aggravated assault—dropped 36 percent from 1994 to 1999. Burglary is down 60 percent since 1980, and juvenile arrest rates for weapons crimes fell by 39 percent from 1993 to 1999. Despite these statistics, tragic events such as school shootings have led the public to perceive an increase in both the severity and frequency of juvenile crimes. A 2000 Gallup Poll revealed that Americans believe juveniles to be responsible for 43 percent of all violent crime in the United States, even though statistics from the Office of Juvenile Justice and Delinquency Prevention (OJJDP) claim that juveniles are responsible for only 12 percent of all violent crime.

Just as Americans disagree on the severity of the problem of juvenile crime, they also debate its causes. Many argue that the proliferation of violence in the media contributes significantly to violent behavior in young people. When Michael Carneal was asked by police if he had ever seen anything similar to his actions before, he replied that he had seen it in the 1995 film *The Basketball Diaries*. The film, which depicts the descent of a promising young poet and basketball player into a sordid life of heroin addiction, contains a dream sequence in which the central character breaks down a door at his high school and kills his classmates with a shotgun. The parents of the three slain girls in Kentucky claim that the violence depicted in the movie— particularly in that scene—influenced Carneal to commit his crime, and they have filed a lawsuit against the makers of the film, Time Warner and Polygram Film. The parents are not alone in their argument, however, as sociologists, psychologists, and even the entertainment industries have begun to examine the amount of violence in the media and its effect on young people.

In 1994, the National Cable Television Association (NCTA) launched the National Television Violence Study (NTVS), which evaluated the content of violent television programming from 1994 to 1997. The study found that the violent content of television shows increased from slightly over one-half of prime time programming to two-thirds of all programming by the end of the study. Seventy-five percent of violent scenes showed no punishment for the characters' aggressive actions. In addition, many of the villains and heroes on television and in movies experience little or no injury from their gunshot wounds, stabbings, or broken limbs. Psychologists claim that the sheer volume of violence depicted in the media teaches children to respond to everyday situations with aggression. Moreover, because the media do not realistically depict the negative consequences of violence, critics assert, young people are further encouraged to imitate the actions of heroic figures on television.

The NTVS study also revealed that juveniles who watch a lot of television seem to be less disturbed by violence in general and are less likely to see anything wrong with it. By the time most young people graduate from high school, they will have witnessed an average of 200,000 acts of violence and 16,000 murders on television and in movies. Experts claim that such exposure to violence decreases a child's sensitivity to another person's pain and suffering. Having seen so many acts of violence, children may lose their capacity for empathy and become less distressed by real acts of violence. Psychologist Leonard Eron concludes that "there can no longer be any doubt that heavy exposure to televised violence is one of the causes of aggressive behavior, crime, and violence in society. The evidence comes from both the laboratory and real-life studies. Television violence affects youngsters of all ages, of both genders, at all socio-economic levels and all levels of intelligence. The effect is not limited to children who are already disposed to being aggressive and is not restricted to this country."

Other experts maintain that there is no conclusive evidence that links media violence to aggression. Jonathan Freedman, a psychology professor at the University of Toronto, claims that factors other than media violence contribute to juvenile aggression and that the scientific evidence is not consistent enough to prove a causal link between fantasy violence and violent behavior: "The scientific evidence does not support the view that exposure to media violence causes aggression. Kids were aggressive long before media or television was around. So there are a lot of reasons why kids can be aggressive. It's an easy out—it's an easy scapegoat." Freedman and others argue that child abuse is a much more conclusive cause of juvenile crime than violent images in the media.

Richard Rhodes, author of *Why They Kill: Discoveries of a Maverick Criminologist*, concurs, claiming that children learn violent behavior from their family and peers, not from violence in the media: "Violence isn't learned from mock violence. There is good evidence . . . that it's learned in personal violent encounters, beginning with the brutalization of children by their parents or their peers." Rhodes and others maintain that a child's interpersonal relationships, not entertainment choices, define his or her perception of acceptable behavior, and that it is the parents' responsibility to teach their children the difference between fantasy violence and reality.

The shooting in Kentucky led to an inquiry by the Federal Trade Commission in 1999 into the marketing practices of the entertainment industries, which found that the television, film, and music industries deliberately marketed products that were inappropriately violent to children under seventeen. In response, the industries agreed to increase their self-regulatory efforts at providing age-appropriate material to young people, but they continue to maintain that fantasy violence does not lead to aggressive behavior in juveniles. Whether violent images in the media contribute to juvenile crime is one of the issues debated in *Juvenile Crime: Opposing Viewpoints*, which contains the following chapters: Are Juvenile Crime and Violence Increasing? What Causes Juvenile Crime and Violence? What Factors Contribute to Gang-Related Juvenile Crime? How Can Juvenile Crime Be Combated? Examination of these topics should give readers an understanding of the various issues surrounding the problem of juvenile crime.

CHAPTER 1

Are Juvenile Crime and Violence Increasing?

Chapter Preface

Appalling reports of juvenile crime and violence are becoming increasingly commonplace. For example, in St. Louis in 1996, a fifteen-year-old pregnant girl was shot and killed on the school bus by a fellow classmate. In Florida, a thirteen-year-old student shot and killed a popular teacher in 2000. In the same year in Washington, a six-year-old boy killed a classmate after an argument.

Media portrayals of events such as these have led some to perceive an increase in youth crime and violence. Further, statistics reveal that a demographic surge of adolescent males may lead to further increases in youth violence, according to criminologist James A. Fox. Fox alleges that murder rates among fourteen- to seventeen-year-old males increased 124 percent from 1986 to 1991, and it is this age group that will increase dramatically by 2005, causing the current level of juvenile crime to skyrocket.

Others contend, however, that incidents of juvenile violence are isolated, and that the media hype such rare crimes to increase ratings and because they lack other material for their news reports. According to Vincent Schiraldi, director of the Justice Policy Institute, "The majority of times teenagers are depicted on the evening news, it is in connection with some form of violence, even though fewer than one half of 1 percent of America's juveniles were arrested for a violent crime in 1996." Media critics allege that excessive coverage of violent juvenile crime causes society to perceive juveniles as more violent than they actually are.

The tragedy of school shootings and juvenile murders is undisputed. Whether or not a wave of remorseless, predatory juveniles will surface is one of the issues debated in the following chapter on juvenile crime and violence.

> "Experts believe that 25 percent of all
> murders committed by the year 2005 will
> be committed by juveniles."

Juvenile Crime and Violence Are Increasing

Steve Macko

In the following viewpoint, Steve Macko argues that juvenile crime is a serious problem that is getting worse. In the late 1980s and early 1990s, the introduction of crack cocaine into American society and the resulting gang and drug wars caused an explosion of juvenile crime and violence. Although statistics show a subsequent decrease in crime rates, experts claim that a demographic surge in adolescent males will cause the existing level of crime and violence to skyrocket, as the most common offenders are males between the ages of fourteen and seventeen. Macko is an editor for the *EmergencyNet News Service*, an independent online news forum.

As you read, consider the following questions:
1. What, according to Macko, is the "revolving door" process?
2. How does the author define the "get tough" approach?
3. What are three of the social problems linked to crime, according to the author?

Excerpted from Steve Macko, "Kids with No Hope, No Fear, No Rules, and No Life Expectancy," *EmergencyNet News Service*, May 18, 1996. Reprinted by permission of *EmergencyNet News Service*, www.emergency.com.

There is a bitter battle over how to combat the nation's fastest-growing crime problem—juvenile offenders. While overall crime statistics in America's largest cities has dropped, there is one category where it has skyrocketed. That category is homicides committed by youths under the age of 17. Between 1984 and 1994, murders committed by youths under 17 tripled. Demographic studies show that there will be a surge in the teen population in the coming years and experts believe that 25 percent of all murders committed by the year 2005 will be committed by juveniles.

Violence (i.e. aggravated assaults) committed with guns by youths has also increased at roughly the same pace as homicides. After years of statistical decline, drug use by teens is also on the rise. None of these statistics would appear to bode well for future.

It now seems that every day we are hearing about horrendous violent crimes being committed by juveniles. The most famous of late was the 6-year-old in northern California who almost beat to death a small baby. The baby suffered brain damage from the attack by the 6-year-old. There is also the case of the 15-year-old pregnant girl who was shot to death by another student in St. Louis. In Miami, two 16-year-old males have been charged with the murder of a Dutch woman tourist who just happened to end up in the wrong neighborhood. A 15-year-old New York boy tried to steal a pair of earrings from a woman. During the attack, the young woman fell to her death under a New York subway train. In Fort Meyers, Florida, a group of teenagers shot and killed a high school band teacher. A police investigation into this group of teens turned up "would-be junior terrorists" that could have rivaled some of the worst terrorist organizations in the world. On Friday, in St. Louis, one 9-year-old and two 11-year-old males were charged with the rape of an 8-year-old female in an overgrown field. Where are they learning this stuff? This has to be learned behavior. [All these attacks occurred in 1996 alone.]

There seems to be growing awareness now of this juvenile crime problem in the United States. Several experts, as well as this publication, have been trying very hard to get the word out. People who have become victims of these young felons are angry and are calling for changes to be made in the juvenile justice system.

It has been a long-standing belief in the United States that juveniles who kill, rape, and rob be treated differently than adult offenders. But this may soon change. In 1899, juvenile courts were established to help protect "juvenile delinquents." But it seems that today, the reasoning for the protection of the youths in the criminal justice system may be outdated and changes need to be made to accommodate these "14-year-old hardened felons." Many critics, today, say that in reality too many hard-core juvenile offenders are arrested, held, and released time-after-time-after-time in a process that is called a revolving door. It seems to only come to an end when a truly heinous crime is committed.

Worse Rather than Better in the Future

Because of the rise in juvenile crime and the experts' predictions that the problem is going to get worse before it gets better, many cities, states and even congress are trying to wrestle with the problem. Tallahassee, Florida, has been experimenting with a couple of different programs to deal with troubled youths. In one case in 1996, Tallahassee Police received a report of a teenager breaking into an auto. Immediately, officers knew their suspect. The suspect was a 16-year-old, who even held a job at a near-by restaurant. This 16-year-old, who was on parole, had been known to commit 32 similar offenses. Officers had kept the suspect tracked on a point scale. He was arrested after he barricaded himself inside an apartment building. Because of his extensive criminal record, prosecutors immediately sent him to trial in an adult court. This can be called the "get-tough" approach.

In another case, in the same city, a softer approach is taken with another known troubled child. A fifth-grader was repeatedly getting into trouble with the law in the summer of 1995. In six weeks, after special classes and counseling that were followed by daily after-school sessions, the child went from "class problem to developing leader." The child was named his school's "student of the month" in January 1996.

So, which is the best approach to take? Because of the grim statistics and depressing stories about problem youths, cities, states and even the federal government are looking at new ways to get a handle on the problem. On the federal end, Congress is considering rewriting a 22-year-old law that provides anti-delinquency aid to states.

In one state, Massachusetts, the House of Representatives has voted that anyone as young as the age of 14 may be tried as an adult in a murder case. The State of Tennessee has now eliminated any minimum age for trying juveniles as adults. In 1995, Oregon lowered its minimum age for someone to be able to be tried as an adult from 14 down to 12-years. Wisconsin went even lower. A child of 10-years-of-age can now be tried as an adult.

Causative Factors

What's the cause of all of this? Statistics show mounting concerns. In the mid-1980's there was a cocaine epidemic. Drug wars between street gangs and drug dealers led to an arms race on American streets. The number of black males aged 14 to 17 is due to rise by 26 percent by the year 2005. Unfortunately, statistics prove that such youths are disproportionately affected by social problems linked historically to crime. These social problems include: the breakdown of the family, poverty and poor education. It really is not surprising that facing these kinds of social problems, inner-city black youths are disproportionately involved in crime.

Sixty-one percent of all juveniles arrested for homicide in 1994 were black. Remember, blacks make up about 12 percent of the overall population in the United States. Fifty-two percent of the murdered victims in 1994 were also black. "Black on Black" crime appears to be a major fact of the statistics.

Criminologist James Alan Fox of Northeastern University in Boston said, "Given our wholesale disinvestment in youth, we will likely have more than 5,000 teen killers per year." The United States averages, currently, about 21,000 homicides per year. The number of youths aged 14 and younger who have been charged with homicide has jumped by 43 percent in the past twenty years.

The thing that worries everyone from police officers to criminologists to the general public are the small number of teens who apparently kill or maim with little or no moral compunction. Cincinnati judge David Grossmann, the president of a national juvenile judges organization, says that he sees a wave of "undisciplined, untutored, unnurtured young people." The Judge added, "Gangs have become the alternative to a nurturing family."

Kathleen Heide is a criminologist and a psychotherapist in Florida. She said that many young murderers "are incapable of empathy." Heide related one case in 1996 where a teen offender shot and paralyzed a jogger who refused to hand over a gold neck chain. When the teen offender was asked what might had been a preferable alternative outcome other than shooting the victim, the teen said, "He could have given me his rope (chain). I asked him twice."

Demographic Surge

At this point in time, the U.S. is due for a demographic double-whammy. Not only are violent teens maturing into even more violent young adults, but they are being succeeded by a new and larger group of teenagers. The same massive baby boom generation that, as teenagers, produced a crime wave in the 1970s has grown up and had children of their own. This "baby boomerang" cohort of youngsters now is reaching adolescence.

By the year 2005, the number of teenagers aged 15–19 will increase by 23% which undoubtedly will bring additional increases in crime and other social ills associated with overpopulation of youth. The population growth will be even more pronounced among minorities. For example, the amount of 15–19-year-olds will rise 28% among blacks and 47% among Hispanics. Given that a large number of these children often grow up in conditions of poverty, many more teenagers will be at risk in the years ahead.

James Alan Fox and Glenn Pierce, *USA Today*, January 1994.

According to John Firman of the International Association of Chiefs of Police, police officers are now encountering more and more "kids with no hope, no fear, no rules and no life expectancy." Princeton University political scientist John Dilulio said that inner-city neighborhoods are raising too many "chaotic, dysfunctional, fatherless, Godless and jobless youths where self-respecting young men literally aspire to get away with murder."

Criminal Justice Response

Some states are getting tough on juvenile offenders. In Arizona, the governor of the state, Fife Symington, is working very hard and is leading a petition drive to abolish the state juvenile court system altogether. The aim is to send the most violent young offenders to adult courts, regardless of age, even if judges, themselves, object. An aide to Governor Symington said, "The current law making everyone under 18 a juvenile is absurd." The aide, who was a former prosecutor, said, "We've had kids arrested ten or fifteen times . . . that has to stop." It is said that people "are standing in line" to sign the governor's petition.

In the United States Congress, many conservatives argue that the current federal anti-delinquency statute is out of date. Many Congressmen only want to send aid to states who try their most violent youths as adults.

But even if we, as a country, do crack down and get tough on these young violent offenders . . . it's still not an easy solution. As Donna Hamparian, a crime consultant in Columbus, Ohio, pointed out—even if we do put more youths behind bars, the projected number of juvenile offenders will probably be so high that "we can't build enough prisons to keep all of them locked up."

> "*The truth about violence in America is that it is falling, not rising.*"

Juvenile Crime and Violence Are Not Increasing

James Glassman

While some argue that recent incidents of school violence represent an increase in youth brutality and crime, others maintain that such occurrences are isolated and infrequent. In the following viewpoint, James Glassman maintains that school shootings fail to reflect a growing trend of juvenile violence, and that statistics instead have shown a substantial decrease in youth crime. Glassman is a columnist for the *Washington Post*.

As you read, consider the following questions:
1. What does the author mean by "a sense of proportion"?
2. What are two reasons the author gives for the substantial press coverage violent incidents receive from the media?
3. How does the author define a "social synecdoche"?

Reprinted from ". . . or a Made-up Menace?" by James Glassman, *Washington Post*, May 26, 1998. Reprinted with permission of the author.

In May 1998, a skinny 15-year-old whose self-described hobbies included "sugared cereal [and] throwing rocks at cars," fired 51 shots into a crowded high school cafeteria in Oregon. Two students died, and 22 were wounded. The suspect, Kipland P. Kinkel, also was accused of killing his parents.

TV broadcasts and newspapers were full of the story. The *New York Times* ran it for three straight days on the front page. President Bill Clinton used his Saturday radio address to decry the "changing culture that desensitizes our children to violence." He asserted that these schoolhouse shootings "are more than isolated incidents."

So they seem. Since October 1997, 14 teachers and students have been murdered.

Let's stipulate that these killings are sickening and that it would be an enormous benefit to humanity to prevent the shooting of a schoolchild from ever happening again. But let's also put these murders into perspective.

Violence Is Decreasing

First, the truth about violence in America is that it is falling, not rising. In fact, the single biggest story since the fall of the Berlin Wall in 1989 is the decline in serious crime—a true man-bites-dog tale. After climbing at a seemingly inexorable pace since the 1970s, crime has dropped—suddenly and broadly, and for reasons that still are unexplained.

From 1993 to 1996, the number of murders fell 20 percent, and just four days before the Oregon shootings, the FBI announced preliminary figures for 1997 that found both murders and robbery down another 9 percent and overall crime off for the sixth straight year. Murders in New York City fell a stunning 22 percent in 1997; in Los Angeles, 20 percent.

"It's hard to think of a social trend of greater significance," wrote Gordon Witkin of *U.S. News & World Report.* He's right. As crime rates have declined, cities—most significantly, New York, where the murder rate is lower than in Kansas City and Charlotte—have revived. Burglary and car-theft rates are now higher in Britain and Sweden than in America. Government, at last, is beginning to accomplish its most important function, which is to protect us so we can pursue happiness in our daily lives.

Maintaining a Sense of Proportion

Second, while the killing of any young person is appalling, a sense of proportion is necessary. The United States has 38 million children between the ages of 10 and 17 and 20,000 secondary schools. In 1994, there were no school shootings in which more than one person was killed; in 1997, there were four; in 1998, two. In 1995, 319 kids aged 10 to 14 were murdered; the homicide rate for seniors aged 70 to 74 is 50 percent higher.

Again, the real story about kids is the opposite of the portrait of chaos and anguish painted in the press. A new study by the National Bureau of Economic Research finds that young people are "getting happier" while "older Americans, by contrast, indicated little change in their degree of happiness."

The Statistical Decrease

California teen murder arrest rate/100,000 age 10–17 by race, 1967–1998

Mike Males and Dan Macallair, *Justice Policy Institute*, 1999.

You have to wonder about the claims of pop psychologists and of President Bill Clinton himself when he says that the rising tide of murders and mayhem on TV, in movies and on video games is turning kids into killers. Indeed, *U.S. News* noted that "juvenile murder arrests declined . . . 14 percent from 1994 to 1995 and another 14 percent from 1995 to

1996." Clinton is going to have to think of a phenomenon other than video gore on which to blame the shootings.

Media Frenzy

Here's one idea: the inordinate play these stories get in the press. Children like Kipland Kinkel are bombs waiting for detonation, and the media, by blaring their exploits on the front pages and the nightly news, may be helping to light the fuse. I'm not in favor of suppression, but I am opposed to obsession, which is what we have now.

Why? Well, one answer may be a crime shortage. At a Harvard symposium recently, one panelist pointed out that local TV news shows have to import violent footage now that local criminals aren't turning out enough products (there were only 43 murders in Boston in 1997, the fewest since 1961).

Another reason is a news shortage. In an era of peace and prosperity, the press finds little to excite the imagination—and prey on the fears—of its audience.

In such an atmosphere, one choice for the press would be to examine larger, long-range problems, such as how to fix Social Security, or why crime rates are falling. Another is to blow individual incidents in small towns in Oregon into national crises.

This is an especially irresponsible approach because most people practice a kind of social synecdoche—they believe that the part equals the whole, that a single shooting (or even four in a year) can mean that child murderers are rampant and some new solution is required. The press consistently fails to put events into context, even when statistics show what's happening in the aggregate.

So, what's the meaning of the schoolhouse murders? Frankly, not much. The meaning of the hysteria over them . . . now, that's worth looking into.

"From overt violent acts to concealed crimes, violence in schools affects everyone— teachers, parents, children and the whole community."

Juvenile Crime Is a Serious Problem in Schools

National Center for Victims of Crime

Several recent school shootings, gang activity, and juvenile drug use have raised public awareness about the safety of schools and their surroundings. Many school districts have implemented such safety strategies as metal detectors and armed security officers in an effort to protect students and faculty from firearms and other weapons. In the following viewpoint, the National Center for Victims of Crime (NCVC) describes some of the dangers and concludes that juvenile crime and violence are a major problem within the public school system. The NCVC is a nonprofit organization dedicated to helping victims of crime rebuild their lives.

As you read, consider the following questions:
1. To what does the NCVC and other researchers attribute the high percentage of juvenile homicide victims in 1991?
2. How does the NCVC define a "hate crime"?
3. What are two features of the National School Safety Center's security plan?

Excerpted from "School of Crime," an informational bulletin published by the National Center for Victims of Crime, Arlington, Virginia. Used with permission.

O ur nation's schools, once a protected haven for learning and growth, are no longer safe for teachers or students in many of our nation's communities.

From overt violent acts, such as homicide and assaults, to concealed crimes, such as child sexual abuse, violence in schools affects everyone—teachers, parents, children and the whole community. Victims of violent crime in the school, like victims elsewhere, may suffer physical ailments, withdrawal from peer relations, and display indifference to learning. They also may be more likely to abuse alcohol or drugs, which contributes to lack of learning, growth and development, and hinders the effective education of children.

Today, the problems in our schools are firearms, weapons, substance abuse and gangs. Many people equate school violence with large urban areas; however, violence has invaded suburban and rural schools as well. Not only public schools, but private schools are also involved.

Firearms

Guns in schools have increased to the point that approximately one in four major school districts now use metal detectors to reduce the number of weapons brought into schools by students. The juvenile offenders who are arrested for weapons violations are sometimes fellow students, and other times non-student peers, who threaten and attack students, administrators and teachers. According to a 1994 survey conducted by the National Parents' Resource Institute for Drug Education, almost one in thirteen (7.4%) of all high school students carried a gun to school in 1993–1994, and 35 percent (35%) threatened to harm another student or a teacher.

According to the Centers for Disease Prevention and Control, guns claimed the lives of 88 percent (88%) of the 15 to 19 year old homicide victims in 1991, and researchers attribute this high percentage to the increased use of guns instead of fists to settle arguments. Gun violence among juveniles also causes countless injuries and disabilities. Research by the National Association of Children's Hospitals and Related Institutions shows that the average cost of treating a child wounded by gunfire is more than $14,000, enough to pay for a year of college. . . .

Drug and Alcohol Abuse

Almost three out of four students reported that drugs were available at school in 1995. While illegal consumption or sale of drugs and alcohol among school children may not, in itself, be violent, such behavior often leads to violent acts. A *National Crime Survey Report* found that 37 percent (37%) of violent crime offenders ages 16 to 19 were perceived by their victims to be under the influence of drugs and/or alcohol.

AMERICA, 1999: WHAT'S WRONG WITH THIS PICTURE?

Horsey. Reprinted by permission of North America Syndicate.

Another survey conducted by the National Parents' Resource Institute for Drug Education found that high school students who carried guns to school in 1993–1994 were 14.5 times more likely to use cocaine, nearly twice as likely to drink alcohol and three times as likely to smoke marijuana as other students. This survey also found that students involved in school and community activities and those whose parents talked to them about drugs' dangers were half as likely to use drugs.

28.4 percent of students in 1995 reported that street gangs were present in their schools compared to 15.3% in 1989. Organized youth gangs are *not* limited to large, inner-city areas as is commonly believed, and membership crosses all racial and ethnic boundaries. According to a survey conducted by the National Parents' Resource Institute for Drug Education, 13.8 percent (13.8%) of American high school students joined a gang during the 1993–1994 school year. With these younger gang members attending school, schools themselves have become prime recruiting grounds. Gang members stake out their turfs in their territory, including the neighborhood school grounds. . . .

Crimes committed against persons because of their ethnic, cultural, religious or socio-economic background or sexual orientation are on the rise in American society. In schools, this can mean discriminatory practices by educators and fellow students, malicious graffiti on walls or lockers, and interpersonal confrontations. Each of these can lead to violence, and all are detrimental to a supportive educational environment. . . .

Homicide

According to the Centers for Disease Prevention and Control, the homicide rate for males ages 15 to 19 jumped from 13 per 100,000 in 1985 to 33 per 100,000 in 1991, a 154 percent (154%) increase. Arrests of juveniles for murder increased by 85 percent (85%) between 1987 and 1991, and multiple-offender homicides involving juvenile offenders have more than doubled since the mid-1980s. When juveniles commit homicide, 64 percent (64%) of their victims are friends, family or acquaintances. . . .

School Safety as a Policy

What can be done to provide a safer school environment? In the National School Safety Center (NCSSC) resource paper, *School Crisis Prevention and Response*, it is noted that courts have held that schools are expected to provide a physical environment conducive to the purposes of an educational institution, although a school may not be expected to ensure nor guarantee the safety of its students. . . .

The National School Safety Center recommends that a security plan be prepared and that the following general security measures be taken to lessen the chances of school violence:

- A local school security committee or task force comprised of school officials should be established by school districts. Planning for needed safety measures and their implementation should be performed by this task force, including regular review of safety and security measures.
- Crime prevention expertise should be developed and greater responsibility taken by school administrators in working with the school board and districts.
- A comprehensive crisis management plan should be developed by schools which incorporates resources available through other community agencies.
- Regular updates on safety plans and in-service training should be conducted to keep school staff informed. The training should include certified staff, classified staff, part-time employees and substitute teachers.
- Volunteers from the community, as well as parents, should be used to help patrol surrounding neighborhoods and supervise the campus before, during and after school.
- Access points to school campuses should be monitored during the school day. Access should be limited where possible. A single visitor entrance should be monitored by a receptionist or security officer and visitors should be required to sign in and wear an identification pass. Delivery entrances should also be monitored closely.
- Students should be taught to report suspicious individuals or unusual activity. They should also be taught to take responsibility for their own safety by learning personal safety and conflict resolution techniques.
- A curriculum committee focusing on teaching students non-violence, pro-social skills, conflict resolution, law-related education, and good decision-making should be established.
- Plans should be made to establish alternative schools to handle problem students. When these offenders are expelled from school there must be other programs in place to keep them off the streets where other violent incidents may be perpetrated.

Efforts such as these require the support of parents, teachers, administrators, social workers, criminal justice professionals and community leaders working together.

*"Isolated incidents of school shootings in no
way change the fact that school is the safest
place in a teenager's world."*

Juvenile Crime Is Not a Serious Problem in Schools

Patrick Welsh

While some argue that public schools are rife with violence
and crime, others contend that recent school shootings are
isolated incidents that have been hyped by the media. Sta-
tistically, according to Patrick Welsh, school violence has
decreased while students face the more relevant dangers of
car accidents, suicide, and eating disorders. In the following
viewpoint, Welsh argues that violence and crime in schools
are the exception in a generally safe environment. Welsh is
an English teacher at T.C. Williams High School in Alexandria, Virginia, and a member of *USA Today*'s board of
contributors.

As you read, consider the following questions:
1. Why was Welsh angered by the perception the
   community had of the violence in his school?
2. Why, according to principal John Porter and officer
   Hassan Aden, do students start fights in front of them?
3. What does Aden claim to be the real key to school safety?

Reprinted from Patrick Welsh, "Are Schools Really Dangerous? Not Mine—and
Not Most Others," *USA Today*, April 18, 2000, by permission of the author.

L ong before the Columbine tragedy in April 1999, there was great concern for the safety of students at the high school where I teach, T.C. Williams in Alexandria, Virginia. The parents of my affluent students were often asked how they could risk sending their children to such a dangerous place.

Students of mine who had transferred in from private schools were warned by teachers and classmates alike about the violence they would encounter in our hallways and bathrooms. When our football team traveled to suburban schools, the police presence usually was increased.

While I always was amused by these perceptions, I also was angered. As I saw it, they flowed from the assumption that schools with a high percentage of minority students (T.C. Williams has 2,000 students, 45% of them black, 27% white and 28% foreign born—20% of whom are Hispanic) were inherently dangerous.

My daily experience in the classrooms and hallways of my school over nearly 30 years totally belied that assumption.

What's ironic to me, and especially to many of my black students, is that Columbine and the major incidents of school violence that have sparked the recent national concern over safety were perpetrated by white kids. To black students, the refrain "We believed it couldn't happen here" coming from Columbine and other communities was code for "We didn't think white kids could do a thing like this."

Says senior Janelle Loving who will be attending NYU in 2001, "Adults associate school violence with black and Hispanic kids. . . . When white kids commit some horribly violent act, people look for excuses. . . . 'He has psychological issues.' Black guys are simply labeled as thugs."

Media Hype

I'm not so cynical as to believe that the current concern over school safety has come from the fact that in the most heinous recent incidents white students were both perpetrators and victims. But there is no question that the hand wringing and political posturing on school violence and the media hype are far out of proportion to the reality.

In April 2000 the Justice Policy Institute, a Washington, D.C., think tank, released "School House Hype: Two Years

Later," a study that shows that from 1998 to 1999 the number of school-related violent deaths decreased 40%, from 43 deaths in 1998 to 26 in 1999.

A 1998 study by the U.S. Centers for Disease Control and Prevention showed that from 1993 to 1997, fights in schools decreased 14%; injuries from fights fell 20%. The number of kids who reported carrying a weapon to school during the previous 30 days dropped 30%.

Granted, a shooting at a school is unthinkable, contrary to everything any civilized community would expect, and it is only natural that several shootings over a two-year period would reverberate across the country.

But just as air travel is still the safest form of transportation despite horrifying crashes, isolated incidents of school shootings in no way change the fact that school is the safest place in a teenager's world.

Principal John Porter and Hassan Aden, the police officer assigned to my school, both told me that kids actually have started fights right in front of them.

Kids Are Safer at School

Tragic, high profile cases of school violence have repeatedly seized the public's attention over the past several years. Despite these incidents, students were about three times more likely to be victims of nonfatal, serious, violent crime away from school than at school, according to a new report on school safety. In 1997, students aged 12 through 18 were victims of about 202,000 incidents of nonfatal serious violent crime at school, and about 636,000 incidents away from school.

Annie Woo, *Safety Zone*, Winter 1999.

"They know we will break it up. . . . So they get the desired effect—acting macho, but having it stopped before it gets too serious, without losing face. If they get into a fight on the street, they know they have too much too lose. . . . That things could escalate way beyond what they want," says Aden.

In Northern Virginia, where I live, scores of teenagers have died in car accidents since 1995; several have committed suicide; others have died from eating disorders. At the same time, there have been only two deaths through violence in those schools. Yet, listening to the media and to politicians, we can't help but draw the conclusion that school violence is the main threat to our children's well-being.

Security Excesses

Lawmakers in my own state seem especially confused on the issue. They just mandated a minute of silence before each school day in 2001 in hopes of curbing violence, while still allowing concealed weapons to be brought into recreation centers and shotguns to be kept in the trunks of students' cars during hunting season.

Throughout the country school security has become an obsession—metal detectors, locker searches—one school system brought in a SWAT team to practice emergency evacuation of shooting victims. Students in the mock exercise actually were evacuated by helicopter.

My school has its own little gimmick—a safety hotline line that allows students to anonymously report any potential trouble they see. Shortly after Columbine, President Bill Clinton visited the school and praised the hotline program although at the time no one had ever used it.

But as Principal John Porter says, "no matter how many precautions you take, you can't necessarily keep someone who really wanted to cause trouble out of a building. We have more than 80 doors and all kinds of windows where someone wanting to get into school most likely could find a way. Even a strongly fortified building like the U.S. Capitol was penetrable by someone who had a grudge."

Adds Officer Aden: "You can have metal detectors and turn a campus into an armed camp with police all over the place, but the real key to school safety is having open lines of communication with students. When kids feel they can talk to adults they trust, they'll come forward to prevent something from happening."

Aden has had gang members and kids on probation warn him of fights in the neighborhoods that could spill over into school.

"Even the toughest kids want to avoid trouble at school; they need caring adults to help them do it," says Aden.

*"In some cases, kids are slain just for 'props'
(as in 'proper respect')—to enhance the
killer's reputation and bragging rights."*

Juveniles Are Becoming Ruthless

Scott Minerbrook

Although youth crime has always existed in some form, many argue that juveniles are performing increasingly vicious and cold-blooded acts of murder and mayhem. In the following viewpoint, Scott Minerbrook contends that child abuse, the threat of gangs and street violence, and an ineffective juvenile justice system combine to create killers without remorse or fear of punishment. Minerbrook is a writer for *U.S. News & World Report* and the author of *Divided to the Vein*, a novel describing the difficulties of growing up biracial.

As you read, consider the following questions:
1. How does Professor James Garbarino compare the symptoms of children in poor neighborhoods to those of war-torn lands?
2. How, according to the author, does witnessing violence affect children?
3. What does the author describe as three effects of the explosion of crack cocaine in the 1980s?

These are the reasons children are dying in America's mean streets at the hands of other children: sneakers and lambskin coats, whispers and trivial insults over menacing looks, scuffles over pocket change and, of course, drug turf. In some cases, kids are slain just for "props" (as in "proper respect")—to enhance the killer's reputation and bragging rights. Not only are the reasons unfathomably trivial but the responses of the killers are chilling; a smirk, a shrug, a coldblooded comment. The killers are "the young and the rootless," says James Alan Fox, dean of criminal justice studies at Northeastern University. And their malign ethos has metastasized to the suburbs, where youthful murder is increasingly common.

Children of War

Heartless killers and habitual criminals have always existed. But the number of killings by younger and younger kids has rarely been higher. There has been scandalously little research into the phenomenon, so experts can offer only a guess at why the number of such crimes has grown so much since the mid-1980s. They think it results from the confluence of several tragic trends: the growth of single-parent families, a sharp rise in child abuse, the arrival of crack cocaine, the escalation of weaponry on the streets and the despair caused by the massive loss of urban manufacturing jobs. The result is an ecology of terror that has turned many poor neighborhoods into war zones. Indeed, psychologist James Garbarino, president of the Erikson Institute in Chicago, says the children of these places show many of the symptoms of kids in war-torn lands, including post-traumatic stress, emotional numbness, depression, anxiety and rage.

A number of studies in recent years show that few of the youths who kill are psychotic. In growing up, many are animated by a chillingly rational response to an environment that is saturated with violence and stress, where it is safe to trust no one and where there is no sense of the future. In the end, these forces create literally hopeless youths subject to what Garbarino calls "terminal thinking." They believe there is nothing but woe in store for them and no solutions to problems except through aggression. Left unmitigated, these habits of mind are increasingly hard to reverse. . . .

Personality and Family

Many developmental specialists agree that violence inter-
rupts the usual growth of empathetic feelings that is necessary for moral reasoning. Ordinarily, such thinking begins at
the age of 3 or 4 and comes from attachments to parents and
others who teach children limits and trust and who demon-
strate love and understanding. Children learn to care for
others and to distinguish right from wrong at this stage by
internalizing the care they receive themselves and applying
it in relationships with others. "If you cut short that process
with an environment of emotional chaos, the value of life
and moral conduct are gone," says Charles Davenport, a
psychiatrist at the Medical College of Ohio.

Many killers are the victims of awful child abuse. In a
study published by the American Academy of Child and
Adolescent Psychiatry in 1988, Dorothy Otnow Lewis
found that 12 of 14 juveniles on death row in four states had
long histories of severe beatings and sexual abuse, sometimes
by drug-addicted parents. These attacks possibly caused
changes in their brain chemistry and prompted violent behavior as the children grew.

In another study, released in 1992, Lewis found that mal-
treatment increased children's inclination to act impulsively,
to be extremely wary of the world and to exhibit "hypervig-
ilance" to potential assaults; it predisposed them to lash out
and to misperceive threats and often caused children to lose
the ability to feel empathy for others. Abuse also diminished
both their judgment and their verbal competence, making
children less able to express what they feel or what happens
to them. "If a person is chronically stressed, the biological
changes that occur make them less able to control their behavior and more likely to lash out," Lewis says.

Witnessing Violence

Other research suggests that witnessing violence can inspire
long-term rage. Robert Pynoos, a trauma psychiatrist at the
University of California at Los Angeles, has found that those
who see their elders unable to control their own aggressiveness often grow up with the same untamed emotions. Sometimes, when young children witness unchecked violence

against someone they know, they later fantasize about intervening to save their loved one and are furious at their inability to stop the violence. The result is that "they don't feel safe in relationships so they say, 'Why should I get into one?'" says Dr. Carl Bell of Chicago's Community Mental Health Council. "They seem glazed and indifferent when, in fact, they are imprisoned in terror."

John Trever. Reprinted with permission.

Murderous violence rarely arises from a single, impulsive moment. Rather, it is often the culmination of years of escalating aggressive acts. The American Psychological Association and the Justice Department released separate studies that show several "developmental pathways" leading boys to violence. As the cruelty progresses, children develop "habits of thought" that rule out calmer ways to settle disputes, according to Ron Slaby, a developmental psychologist who teaches at Harvard University. Most commonly, it starts with stubborn behavior and defiance and progresses between the ages of 8 and 12 to annoying or bullying others. Between ages 12 and 14, it blossoms into minor antisocial behavior like lying or shoplifting and fighting with other boys. Finally, it grows into full-blown, almost relentless violence. On the other hand, Justice Department researchers found that the brave kids who avoided getting into trouble were those who had strong parental supervision, attachments to parents and consistent discipline.

Street Pressures

No single event has contributed more to the recent contagion of violence than the wide availability of crack cocaine in American cities by the mid-to-late 1980s. It inspired the explosive growth of gangs, which became surrogate families to the emotionally wounded children of desolate communities. The lure of unimaginable wealth attracted many of the best, brightest, most enterprising and most charismatic young men to the drug trade—and also those who looked up to them. The drug itself prompted some to kill without remorse while high and made others desperate enough to do anything to find money for the next hit. Finally, the drug profits fueled a prodigious arms race on America's streets; that led competitors to solidify markets or settle differences with an awesome toll in bloodshed.

It was inevitable that bystanders would be caught in the crossfire. A 1992 study of South Side Chicago high school students between the ages of 13 and 18 reported that 47 percent had seen a stabbing, 61 percent had witnessed a shooting, 45 percent had seen someone get killed and 25 percent had experienced all three. "With these children's nerves on edge under constant threat," argues Bell, "it is clear that some will become deeply depressed, others will try to cope and others will become perpetrators.". . .

National Forces

Beyond family and community horrors, many experts say there are larger trends that abet the rise of coldblooded killers. There are the penal policies that allow many of the most violent criminals to return to their homes well before their sentences are served; many are treated as conquering heroes and resume their criminal ways. Then there's the easy access to handguns in many neighborhoods—even for the very young. There's an entertainment industry that each year pumps thousands of images of violence into the homes of kids who already suffer from poor or nonexistent parenting. And not least, there's the loss of millions of urban manufacturing jobs that are no longer available to kids willing to work to avoid lives of crime.

These findings highlight the need for early intervention to help children conquer their environment. Researchers have found that kids as young as 7 can learn to heal themselves by telling stories about the violence they have suffered. And some experts think older kids can be turned away from crime when they are forced to confront directly what violence does to others.

The federal government recently launched massive research that will try to determine how violent behavior can be short-circuited. The results will come none too soon. By the year 2005, the number of 15- to-19-year-olds—the most violence-prone age group—will increase by 23 percent. Unless a way is found to break the vicious cycle of violence, many fear that will mean the emergence of an even larger group of stone killers.

"The image of an army of sociopathic teen 'super-predators' ready to rise up against the citizenry is the product of some fancy special effects."

Juveniles Are Unfairly Blamed for Increasing Crime and Violence

Ira Glasser

Depictions of juvenile crime in the media have led some to perceive a growing trend in youth violence and brutality. In the following viewpoint, the executive director of the American Civil Liberties Union (ACLU), Ira Glasser, contends that this perception is unfounded, as statistics reflect a decrease in juvenile crime. Glasser argues that the real problem confronting children is poverty, not juvenile crime and violence.

As you read, consider the following questions:

1. According to the author, what would the "Violent Youth Predator Act of 1996" mandate?
2. What does the author consider to be the real purpose behind "scapegoating children"?
3. As cited by the author, what does the "family values crowd" consider to be the fate of illegitimate girls and boys?

Taking their cue from the blockbuster movie *Twister*, politicians are warning us about an impending storm— a storm of "youth violence."

Over the next 15 years, according to a recent fact sheet produced by the House Subcommittee on Crime, "the number of teenagers will soar to the highest level in American history." Brace yourself, we are warned, for the "coming storm of violent juvenile crime."

The image of an army of sociopathic teen "super-predators" ready to rise up against the citizenry is the product of some fancy special effects, even fancier than those found in "Twister." But a storm of youth violence isn't brewing on the horizon any more than the actors up on the movie screen were fleeing a real tornado.

Exaggerated Predictions

Contrary to the Subcommittee's "facts," scientific population projections show that while the number of young people between 15 and 24—the crime-prone years—will increase in the next decade, this increase will not exceed that for 1980. In other words, there will be a bulge, not a "storm" or even a high wind, and it won't be unprecedented.

But that hasn't stopped Congress from considering the "Violent Youth Predator Act of 1996." The Act would mandate automatic adult prosecution of children as young as 13, encourage states to hold parents criminally responsible for their children's acts, open up juvenile arrest records to the public, and, for the first time, allow for children to be housed with adult prisoners. [The Act did not pass the House of Representatives in 1996.]

These measures sound tough indeed, at a time when competition for who can sound toughest on crime is practically an Olympic sport. But what does it mean to be "tough" on crime? If being tough means being effective, few politicians have been tough. If it means sounding tough but being ineffective, they've all been tough.

Take the "get tough" proposal to throw children as young as 13 in jail with adults. Recent studies, cited on *Nightline* and elsewhere, show that juvenile offenders who serve time in adult prisons have a higher recidivism rate than those who serve time in juvenile facilities geared towards prevention. But scapegoating children leads to public policies that have everything to do with placating an anxious public, and nothing to do with reality.

Poverty

The sponsors of this act know what the real problem is. Only days before this legislation was announced with great fanfare, the results of the non-profit Luxembourg Income Study were released: the United States has the highest child poverty rate in the developed world—26 percent. This is the real problem that our elected leaders are shrinking from confronting.

Renaming Juvenile Delinquents

Media rhetoric appears to color the public perception of delinquency and youth violence. The news media have picked up on contemporaneous political rhetoric, using terms such as "super predators," "youthful predators," "teen killers," "young thugs," and the like to describe the youthful delinquents of the 1990s. Similarly, the language used to describe juvenile activity has shifted subtly, but dramatically. "Juvenile delinquency" has been transformed to "juvenile crime," "children" increasingly became "juveniles," "juvenile detention homes" turned into "juvenile jails," and "training schools" became "juvenile prisons."

Robert E. Shepherd, "Annual Report of the Coalition for Juvenile Justice," 1997.

Instead, they're turning children, or more accurately, poor children, into America's latest scapegoats. Children are politically defenseless: they can't vote, and they are now being blamed for everything from crime to the breakdown of the family. Ignoring social and economic causes, their circumstances are blamed on individual moral failure. Poor teenagers, we are told over and over again, are uneducated, lazy, irresponsible, crime-prone and violent. (Where have we heard that before?)

Add "illegitimate" to the list, too. According to the so-called family values crowd, "illegitimate" children are more numerous than ever. What's more, if they are born female, they grow up to be unwed teenage mothers who have more "illegitimate" children. And if they are born male, they grow up to be—you guessed it—super-predators.

It should surprise no one that the current demonization of children is based on exaggeration, not fact. The rate of babies born to unwed black teenagers is the same today as it was in 1970: 80 per 1,000 unmarried teenagers. And the crime rate is, and always has been, affected mainly by the proportion of the population that is young and male—and bereft of hope or a stake in the future.

It should surprise no one, either, that it's all been said before. In 1872, during an earlier period of rapid economic and social change, one commentator described the same ineluctable process: "All the neglect and bad education and evil example of a poor class tend to form others, who, as they mature, swell the ranks of ruffians and criminals. So, at length, a great multitude of ignorant, untrained, passionate, irreligious boys and young men are formed. . . ."

Scapegoating Kids

The government's reflexive response to such "evil," then as now, is to punish rather than address the underlying problems. Politicians are falling all over themselves to come up with "tougher" (read: ineffective) measures—like the "Violent Youth Predator Act"—for dealing with today's "ignorant, untrained and passionate" kids.

In a speech on "basic values," Bob Dole referred to the "plague of illegitimacy" that he says is sweeping the country. Dole also supports uniforms and curfews, plus locking up juvenile offenders in adult prisons and punishing unwed teenage mothers by cutting off their welfare benefits. President Bill Clinton, posturing as the stern-but-fair First Daddy, goes out of his way to endorse school uniforms and curfews. And it's still early in the [presidential] campaign.

Scapegoats serve a purpose. They are potent symbols used to divert an anxious public's attention away from real problems. They are also an occasion to pass all kinds of repressive laws that threaten everybody's rights. Curfews, for instance, are applied to all teenagers, not just the handful that commit crimes. Politicians, anxious to be re-elected, create a diversion to appear tough, but let the real problems fester. They aren't interested in long-term solutions, just quick fixes.

When you strip away the "special effects"—the inflamed rhetoric, the skewed statistics, and the ineffective "solutions"—what you are left with is an empty sound stage. Not much of a show, is it?

Periodical Bibliography

The following articles have been selected to supplement the diverse views presented in this chapter. Addresses are provided for periodicals not indexed in the *Readers' Guide to Periodical Literature*, the *Alternative Press Index*, the *Social Sciences Index*, or the *Index to Legal Periodicals and Books*.

Terry Carter — "Equality with a Vengeance: Violent Crimes and Gang Activity by Girls Skyrocket," *American Bar Association Journal*, November 1999. Available from the American Bar Association, 750 North Lakeshore Dr., Chicago, IL 60611.

John J. Dilulio — "How to Deal with the Youth Crime Wave," *Weekly Standard*, September 16, 1996. Available from 1211 Avenue of the Americas, New York, NY 10036.

James Alan Fox and Glenn Pierce — "American Killers Are Getting Younger (the Young Desperados)," *USA Today*, January 1994.

Ted Gest and Dorian Friedman — "The New Crime Wave," *U.S. News & World Report*, August 29, 1994.

Stephen J. Ingley — "Just the Facts," *American Jails*, March/April 1998. Available from 2053 Day Rd., Suite 100, Hagerstown, MD 21740.

Anne C. Lewis — "Lay Off the Kids," *Phi Delta Kappan*, January 4, 1997.

Mark H. Moore and Michael Tonry — "Youth Violence in America," *National Institute of Justice News*, April 1999. Available from 810 Seventh St. NW, Washington, DC 20531.

Katrina Onstad — "What Are We Afraid Of?" *Saturday Night*, March 1997.

Michael Rezendes — "Number of Youths in Custody Up," *Boston Globe*, March 1997. Available from 135 Morrisey Blvd., PO Box 2378, Boston, MA 02107-2378.

David Sarasohn — "Home Alone: Just Kids and All That Fear," *Oregonian*, June 20, 1999. Available from 1320 Broadway SW, Portland, OR 97201.

Vincent Schiraldi — "Hyping Juvenile Crime—A Media Staple," *Christian Science Monitor*, November 6, 1997. Available from One Norway St., Boston, MA 02115.

Howard N. Snyder   "Violent Juvenile Crime: The Number of Violent Juvenile Offenders Declines," *Corrections Today*, April 1999. Available from American Correctional Association, 4380 Forbes Blvd., Lanham, MD 20706-4322.

Jacques Steinberg   "Storm Warning: The Coming Crime Wave Is Washed Up," *The New York Times*, January 3, 1999.

David Whitman and Josh Chetwynd   "The Youth Crisis," *U.S. News & World Report*, May 5, 1997.

Annie Woo   "Violence, Crime Declining at School," *Safety Zone*, Winter 1999. Available from National Resource Center for Safe Schools (NRCSS), 101 Southwest Main, Suite 500, Portland, OR 97204.

CHAPTER 2

What Are the Causes of Juvenile Crime and Violence?

Chapter Preface

Among the many theories debated regarding the causes of juvenile crime and violence—including genetic predisposition, environmental influence, violent images in the media, poverty, and single-parent families—one of the most controversial is whether the availability of guns in American society contributes to juvenile crime. While many argue that the presence of large numbers of guns increases the risk of youth violence and fatalities, others contend that guns protect law-abiding citizens from armed criminals.

According to Eric Lotke, a research associate at the National Center on Institutions and Alternatives, and Vincent Schiraldi, the executive director of the Center on Juvenile and Criminal Justice, in 1987 "the number of juvenile homicides with a firearm started to spiral upwards while the number of non-firearm homicides stayed steady or decreased." Lotke, Schiraldi, and others contend that guns have led to higher rates of violence because they have replaced less fatal weapons. While juveniles used to fight with fists and knives, they now resolve disputes with lethal firearms. And because guns can be used from a distance, they make killing less confrontational and therefore easier.

Defenders of gun ownership, however, contend that firearms protect innocent citizens from violent criminals. According to Paul H. Blackman, researcher for the National Rifle Association, "Guns [are] most commonly used for protection against burglary, assault, and robbery." He maintains that more lives are saved through the lawful use of firearms than are lost. Advocates claim that guns also reduce the risk of victimization by providing law-abiding citizens with adequate self-defense against criminals who obtain guns illegally.

The relationship between the availability of guns and youth violence is just one of the issues debated in the following chapter on the causes of juvenile crime.

"You need a particular environment imposed on a particular biology to turn a child into a killer."

Why the Young Kill

Sharon Begley

A recent concept in the debate over the causes of violent behavior combines the existing arguments that either biological or environmental factors are to blame for juvenile crime. Experts are now considering that some children are born with a predisposition to violence that can either be reinforced or suppressed by his or her caregivers. In the following viewpoint, Sharon Begley makes this argument, claiming that a specific biology and a specific environment combine to produce juvenile violence. Begley is a science writer and senior editor for *Newsweek* magazine.

As you read, consider the following questions:

1. What does the author cite as two arguments against the attempts to trace violence to biology?
2. According to the author, what is the difference between antisocial aggressors and hostile, impulsive aggressors?
3. How does the author describe boys who feel abandoned or lacking in unconditional love?

The temptation, of course, is to seize on one cause, one single explanation for Littleton, and West Paducah, and Jonesboro and all the other towns that have acquired iconic status the way "Dallas" or "Munich" did for earlier generations. Surely the cause is having access to guns. Or being a victim of abuse at the hands of parents or peers. Or being immersed in a culture that glorifies violence and revenge. But there isn't one cause. And while that makes stemming the tide of youth violence a lot harder, it also makes it less of an unfathomable mystery. Science has a new understanding of the roots of violence that promises to explain why not every child with access to guns becomes an Eric Harris or a Dylan Klebold, and why not every child who feels ostracized, or who embraces the Goth esthetic, goes on a murderous rampage. The bottom line: you need a particular environment imposed on a particular biology to turn a child into a killer.

It should be said right off that attempts to trace violence to biology have long been tainted by racism, eugenics and plain old poor science. The turbulence of the 1960s led some physicians to advocate psychosurgery to "treat those people with low violence thresholds," as one 1967 letter to a medical journal put it. In other words, lobotomize the civil-rights and antiwar protesters. And if crimes are disproportionately committed by some ethnic groups, then finding genes or other traits common to that group risks tarring millions of innocent people. At the other end of the political spectrum, many conservatives view biological theories of violence as the mother of all insanity defenses, with biology not merely an explanation but an excuse. The conclusions emerging from interdisciplinary research in neuroscience and psychology, however, are not so simple minded as to argue that violence is in the genes, or murder in the folds of the brain's frontal lobes. Instead, the picture is more nuanced, based as it is on the discovery that experience rewires the brain. The dawning realization of the constant back-and-forth between nature and nurture has resurrected the search for the biological roots of violence.

Early experiences seem to be especially powerful: a child's brain is more malleable than that of an adult. The dark side of the zero-to-3 movement, which emphasizes the huge potential for learning during this period, is that the young brain also is extra vulnerable to hurt in the first years of life. A child who suffers repeated "hits" of stress—abuse, neglect, terror—experiences physical changes in his brain, finds Dr. Bruce Perry of Baylor College of Medicine. The incessant flood of stress chemicals tends to reset the brain's system of fight-or-flight hormones, putting them on hair-trigger alert. The result is the kid who shows impulsive aggression, the kid who pops the classmate who disses him. For the outcast, hostile confrontations—not necessarily an elbow to the stomach at recess, but merely kids vacating en masse when he sits down in the cafeteria—can increase the level of stress hormones in his brain. And that can have dangerous consequences. "The early environment programs the nervous system to make an individual more or less reactive to stress," says biologist Michael Meaney of McGill University. "If parental care is inadequate or unsupportive, the [brain] may decide that the world stinks—and it better be ready to meet the challenge." This, then, is how having an abusive parent raises the risk of youth violence: it can change a child's brain. Forever after, influences like the mean-spiritedness that schools condone or the humiliation that's standard fare in adolescence pummel the mind of the child whose brain has been made excruciatingly vulnerable to them.

In other children, constant exposure to pain and violence can make their brain's system of stress hormones unresponsive, like a keypad that has been pushed so often it just stops working. These are the kids with antisocial personalities. They typically have low heart rates and impaired emotional sensitivity. Their signature is a lack of empathy, and their sensitivity to the world around them is practically nonexistent. Often they abuse animals: Kip Kinkel, the 15-year-old who killed his parents and shot 24 schoolmates last May, had a history of this; Luke Woodham, who killed three schoolmates and wounded seven at his high school in Pearl, Miss., in 1997, had previously beaten his dog with a club, wrapped it in a bag and set it on fire. These are also the adolescents who do not respond to punishment: nothing hurts. Their ability to feel, to react, has died, and so has their conscience. Hostile, impulsive aggressors usually feel sorry afterward. Antisocial aggressors don't feel at all. Paradoxically, though, they often have a keen sense of injustices aimed at themselves.

When Things Go Wrong

Early development does not always proceed in a way that encourages child curiosity, creativity and self-confidence. For some children, early experiences are neither supportive nor predictable. The synapses that develop in the brain are created in response to chronic stress, or other types of abuse and neglect. And, when children are vulnerable to these risks, problematic early experiences can lead to poor outcomes.

For example, some children are born with the tendency to be irritable, impulsive and insensitive to emotions in others. When these child characteristics combine with adult caregiving that is withdrawn and neglectful, children's brains can wire in ways that may result in unsympathetic child behavior. When these child characteristics combine with adult caregiving that is angry and abusive, children's brains can wire in ways that result in violent and overly aggressive child behavior. If the home environment teaches children to expect danger instead of security, then poor outcomes may occur.

Sara Gable and Melissa Hunting, *Human Environmental Sciences*, January 31, 2000.

Inept parenting encompasses more than outright abuse, however. Parents who are withdrawn and remote, neglectful and passive, are at risk of shaping a child who (absent a compensating source of love and attention) shuts down emotionally. It's important to be clear about this: inadequate parenting short of Dickensian neglect generally has little ill effect on most children. But to a vulnerable baby, the result of neglect can be tragic. Perry finds that neglect impairs the development of the brain's cortex, which controls feelings of belonging and attachment. "When there are experiences in early life that result in an underdeveloped capacity [to form relationships]," says Perry, "kids have a hard time empathizing with people. They tend to be relatively passive and perceive themselves to be stomped on by the outside world."

These neglected kids are the ones who desperately seek a script, an ideology that fits their sense of being humiliated and ostracized. Today's pop culture offers all too many dangerous ones, from the music of Rammstein to the game of Doom. Historically, most of those scripts have featured males. That may explain, at least in part, why the murderers are Andrews and Dylans rather than Ashleys and Kaitlins, suggests Deborah Prothrow-Smith of the Harvard School of Public Health. "But girls are now 25 percent of the adolescents arrested for violent crime," she notes. "This follows the media portrayal of girl superheroes beating people up," from Power Rangers to Xena. Another reason that the schoolyard murderers are boys is that girls tend to internalize ostracism and shame rather than turning it into anger. And just as girls could be the next wave of killers, so could even younger children. "Increasingly, we're seeing the high-risk population for lethal violence as being the 10- to 14-year-olds," says Richard Lieberman, a school psychologist in Los Angeles. "Developmentally, their concept of death is still magical. They still think it's temporary, like little Kenny in 'South Park'." Of course, there are loads of empty, emotionally unattached girls and boys. The large majority won't become violent. "But if they're in a violent environment," says Perry, "they're more likely to."

There seems to be a genetic component to the vulnerability that can turn into antisocial-personality disorder. It is only a tiny bend in the twig, but depending on how the child grows up, the bend will be exaggerated or straightened out. Such aspects of temperament as "irritability, impulsivity, hyperactivity and a low sensitivity to emotions in others are all biologically based," says psychologist James Garbarino of Cornell University, author of the upcoming book "Lost Boys: Why Our Sons Turn Violent and How We Can Save Them." A baby who is unreactive to hugs and smiles can be left to go her natural, antisocial way if frustrated parents become exasperated, withdrawn, neglectful or enraged. Or that child can be pushed back toward the land of the feeling by parents who never give up trying to engage and stimulate and form a loving bond with her. The different responses of parents produce different brains, and thus behaviors. "Behavior is the result of a dialogue between your brain and your experiences," concludes Debra Niehoff, author of the recent book "The Biology of Violence." "Although people are born with some biological givens, the brain has many blank pages. From the first moments of childhood the brain acts as a historian, recording our experiences in the language of neurochemistry."

There are some out-and-out brain pathologies that lead to violence. Lesions of the frontal lobe can induce apathy and distort both judgment and emotion. In the brain scans he has done in his Fairfield, Calif., clinic of 50 murderers, psychiatrist Daniel Amen finds several shared patterns. The structure called the cingulate gyrus [CG], curving through the center of the brain, is hyperactive in murderers. The CG acts like the brain's transmission, shifting from one thought to another. When it is impaired, people get stuck on one thought. Also, the prefrontal cortex, which seems to act as the brain's super-visor, is sluggish in the 50 murderers. "If you have violent thoughts that you're stuck on and no super-visor, that's a prescription for trouble," says Amen, author of "Change Your Brain/Change Your Life." The sort of damage he finds can result from head trauma as well as exposure to toxic substances like alcohol during gestation.

Children who kill are not, with very few exceptions, amoral. But their morality is aberrant. "I killed because people like me are mistreated every day," said pudgy, bespectacled Luke Woodham, who murdered three students. "My whole life I felt outcasted, alone." So do a lot of adolescents. The difference is that at least some of the recent school killers felt emotionally or physically abandoned by those who should love them. Andrew Golden, who was 11 when he and Mitchell Johnson, 13, went on their killing spree in Jonesboro, Ark., was raised mainly by his grandparents while his parents worked. Mitchell mourned the loss of his father to divorce.

Unless they have another source of unconditional love, such boys fail to develop, or lose, the neural circuits that control the capacity to feel and to form healthy relationships. That makes them hypersensitive to perceived injustice. A sense of injustice is often accompanied by a feeling of abject powerlessness. An adult can often see his way to restoring a sense of self-worth, says psychiatrist James Gilligan of Harvard Medical School, through success in work or love. A child usually lacks the emotional skills to do that. As one killer told Garbarino's colleague, "I'd rather be wanted for murder than not wanted at all."

That the Littleton massacre ended in suicide may not be a coincidence. As Michael Carneal was wrestled to the ground after killing three fellow students in Paducah in 1997, he cried out, "Kill me now!" Kip Kinkel pleaded with the schoolmates who stopped him, "Shoot me!" With suicide "you get immortality," says Michael Flynn of John Jay College of Criminal Justice. "That is a great feeling of power for an adolescent who has no sense that he matters."

The good news is that understanding the roots of violence offers clues on how to prevent it. The bad news is that ever more children are exposed to the influences that, in the already vulnerable, can produce a bent toward murder. Juvenile homicide is twice as common today as it was in the mid-1980s. It isn't the brains kids are born with that has changed in half a generation; what has changed is the ubiquity of violence, the easy access to guns and the glorification of revenge in real life and in entertainment. To deny the role of these influences is like denying that air pollution triggers childhood asthma. Yes, to develop asthma a child needs a specific, biological vulnerability. But as long as some children have this respiratory vulnerability—and some always will—then allowing pollution to fill our air will make some children wheeze, and cough, and die. And as long as some children have a neurological vulnerability—and some always will—then turning a blind eye to bad parenting, bullying and the gun culture will make other children seethe, and withdraw, and kill.

"While violence may be part of everyone's behavioral repertoire, the temptations to do it are embedded with social networks that more or less make this kind of behavior seem acceptable at the moment."

Environmental Factors Contribute to Juvenile Crime and Violence

Tom O'Connor

Experts on juvenile crime have long debated whether violence is rooted in biological factors, such as birth defects or genetic anomalies, or environmental factors, as in social and economic hardship or family influence. In the following viewpoint, Tom O'Connor argues that although everyone is born with a potential for violence, violent behavior is learned and reinforced by the influences of a child's family and environment, such as poor, gang-infested neighborhoods where guns and drugs are plentiful. Tom O'Connor is an assistant professor of justice studies at North Carolina Wesleyan College.

As you read, consider the following questions:
1. What does the author claim are two main "products of poverty"?
2. What are "neighborhood" factors of juvenile crime, according to O'Connor?
3. What does O'Connor mean by the "catharsis" and "brutalization" effects of media violence?

Reprinted, with permission, from Tom O'Connor, "Juvenile Offenders and Troubled Teens," *MegaLinks in Criminal Justice*, downloaded November 14, 2000, from http://faculty.ncwc.edu/toconnor/juvjusp.htm. Last updated 3/1/00.

O ver the years, criminologists have put forth a wide variety of motives for what causes crime. People who deal with young people cite the following root conditions: poverty, family factors, the environment, media influence, and declining social morality. These will be taken up in order:

Poverty

Although it is considered passe to say poverty causes crime, the fact is that nearly 22 percent of children under the age of eighteen live in poverty. Poverty, in absolute terms, is more common for children than for any other group in society. Ageism, they say, is the last frontier in the quest for economic equality. Adolescents from lower socioeconomic status (SES) families regularly commit more violence than youth from higher SES levels. Social isolation and economic stress are two main products of poverty, which has long been associated with a number of D-words like disorganization, dilapidation, deterioration, and despair. Pervasive poverty undermines the relevance of school and traditional routes of upward mobility. The way police patrol poverty areas like an occupying army only reinforces the idea that society is the enemy whom they should hate. Poverty breeds conditions that are conducive to crime.

Family Factors

One of the most reliable indicators of juvenile crime is the proportion of fatherless children. The primary role of fathers in our society is to provide economic stability, act as role models, and alleviate the stress of mothers. Marriage has historically been the great civilizer of male populations, channeling predatory instincts into provider/protector impulses. Economically, marriage has always been the best way to multiply capital, with the assumption being that girls from poorer families better themselves by marrying upward. Then, of course, there are all those values of love, honor, cherish, and obey encapsulated in the marriage tradition. Probably the most important thing that families impart to children is the emphasis upon individual accountability and responsibility in the forms of honesty, commitment, loyalty, respect and work ethic.

There may be other ways to accomplish these things, but

the traditional vehicle for them, marriage, has been in sharp decline over the last four decades. In 1996, the number of children being raised in single-parent families rose to about 18 million. Divorce accounted for most of this, and it is generally accepted that about 50 percent of American marriages end in divorce. The American divorce rate is the highest of any known society in history. Another contributing factor is the number of out-of-wedlock children. This rate is running at about 33 percent of all childbirths, and at a higher 68 percent for African American babies (32 percent for Latinos, 21 percent for whites). Political pundits claim these figures show "the breakdown of the family structure," and put words like "unwed" and "mother" together to create convenient scapegoats, but social scientists argue against any automatic conclusions about the effects of family breakdown.

Most of the broken home literature, for example, shows only weak or trivial effects, like skipping school or home delinquency. Another area, the desistance literature, shows only that children from two-parent families age-out of crime earlier. In fact, there is more evidence supportive of the hypothesis that a stepparent in the home increases delinquency, or that abuse and neglect in fully intact families lead to a cycle of violence. To complicate matters, there are significant gender, race, and SES interaction effects. Females from broken homes commit certain offenses while males from broken homes commit other kinds of offenses. Few conclusions can be reached about African American males, but tentative evidence suggests stepparenting can be of benefit to them. SES differences actually show that the broken home is less important in producing delinquency among lower-class youth than youth from higher social classes. Most research results are mixed, and no clear causal family factors have emerged to explain the correlation between fatherlessness and crime, but it is certainly unfair to blame single mothers, their parenting skills, or their economic condition for what are obviously more complex social problems.

The Environment

Unless we are willing to believe that testosterone (a male stimulation-seeking hormone) causes crime, the only feasible explanations left are environmental ones. The heredity-environment debate in explaining juvenile crime is shaped by divided opinions about what factors are really important: genetic tendencies, birth complications, and brain chemicals, on one side; and being a victim of abuse, witnessing domestic battering, and learned behaviors, on the other side. The idea that all behavior is learned behavior is associated with environmental explanations. Sure, everyone has a potential for violence, but we learn how to do it (in all its different forms) from observing others do it. In fact, most of us are suckers for observing violence, glamorizing it to the point where we like more and different forms of it every day, in the news, on TV shows, in action movies. So when you're talking about reducing the need to see violence on TV, you're really talking biology or psychology. The study of environmental factors, on the other hand, is concerned primarily with social considerations. While violence may be part of everyone's behavioral repertoire, the temptations (triggers, cues) to do it are embedded (lodged, locked, firmly put in place) with social networks (relationships and situations) that more or less make this kind of behavior seem acceptable at the moment.

The unfortunate truth is that, in many places, there are a growing number of irresistible temptations and opportunities for juveniles to use violence. Brute, coercive force has become an acceptable substitute, even a preferred substitute, for ways to resolve conflicts and satisfy needs. Think of it as the schoolyard bully who says "Meet me in the parking lot at 4:30." Under circumstances like these, the peer pressure and reward systems are so arranged that fighting seems like the only way out.

Now think for a moment about the crucial importance of peer groups: whether there are people who would respect you for standing up to fight, or whether there are people important to you that would definitely not approve of your fighting. What environmental learning theorists are saying is that there are fewer and fewer friends available to help you see the error of your ways in deciding to fight.

Most of the recent research in this area revolves around "neighborhood" factors, such as the presence of gangs, illicit drug networks, high levels of transiency, lack of informal supports, etc. Gang-infested neighborhoods, in particular, have no effective means of providing informal supports that would help in resisting the temptations to commit crime. Such neighborhoods would more likely have an informal encouragement policy, with five or more places where you could buy a gun and drugs available to give you the courage to use the gun. Firearms- and drug-related homicides have increased over 150 percent in recent years, and the clearest drug-violence connection is for selling drugs because illicit drug distribution networks are extremely violent.

Social Implications

If genetic factors play as little part in causing violent behaviour as presently seems to be the case, the social implications are far reaching. In theory it means that if the environmental causes of violence can be identified and if they are of a kind that can be influenced by social and economic policies, then a society in which violence is largely nonexistent is feasible. Property crime emerges from [research] as having a genetic component and it should follow that it will be less affected by social policies. However, it seems improbable that any genetic propensity to steal could account for the huge national and cross-national variations in rates of theft. The tendency to steal is almost certainly largely determined by environmental conditions—such as not having much money. Studies of the relationship between the business cycle and rates of stealing show that rates of this crime are sensitive to environmental influences.

Oliver James, *Juvenile Violence in a Winner-Loser Culture*, 1995.

In such neighborhoods, families, school authorities, and even community organizations are often incapable of providing any protection for children. There are no peer-level social supports to reinforce the conventional lifestyles that these agencies want their children to emulate. The reality of street life, its illicit economy, and quick and easy pathways to success and prestige through violence and crime all offer rewards that offset the risks associated with these activities. And, even if a child experiences the risks of street life firsthand, like by getting shot or stabbed, this only reinforces the child's desire for more exposure to the learning of street life, to do better next time by listening more closely to delinquent peers and not to the advice of legitimate authorities. Victimization and perpetration go hand in hand. This is what is meant when criminologists say that the best predictor of future delinquency is past behavior, or age of onset. The strongest (primacy) effect is when violence is modeled, encouraged, and rewarded for the first time. It determines the type of friends one chooses, which in turn determines what behaviors will be subsequently modeled, established, and reinforced.

Media Influence

Popular explanations of juvenile crime often rest on ideas about the corrupting influence of television, movies, music videos, video games, rap/hip hop music, or the latest scapegoat du jour, computer games like Doom or Quake. The fact is that TV is much more pervasive, and has become the *de facto* babysitter in many homes, with little or no parental monitoring. Where there is strong parental supervision in other areas, including the teaching of moral values and norms, the effect of prolonged exposure to violence on TV is probably quite minimal. When TV becomes the sole source of moral norms and values, this causes problems. Our nation's children watch an astonishing 19,000 hours of TV by the time they finish high school, much more time than all their classroom hours put together since first grade. By eighteen, they will have seen 200,000 acts of violence, including 40,000 murders. Every hour of prime time television carries six to eight acts of violence. Most surveys show that around 80 percent of American parents think there is too much violence on television.

Most of the scientific research in this area revolves around tests of two hypotheses: the catharsis effect, and the brutalization effect; but I am giving this area of research more credit than it deserves because it is not that neatly organized into two hypotheses. Catharsis means that society gets it out of their system by watching violence on TV, and brutalization means we become so desensitized it doesn't bother us anymore, but there are also "imitation" hypotheses, "sleeper" effects, and lagged-time correlations. The results of research in this area are too mixed to give any adequate guidance, and it may well be that social science is incapable of providing us with any good causal analysis in this area. Only anecdotal evidence of a few cases of direct influence exist.

Since the early 1990s, a number of films, music videos, and rap music lyrics have come out depicting gang life, drugs, sex, and violence. Watching or listening to these items gives you the feeling that the filmmakers or musicians really know what they're talking about and tell it like it is, but there have been unfortunate criminogenic effects. In 1992, for example, 144 law enforcement officers were killed in the line of duty. That year, four juveniles wounded Las Vegas police officers, and the rap song *Cop Killer* was implicated. At trial, the killers admitted that listening to the song gave them a sense of duty and purpose. During apprehension, the killers sang the lyrics at the police station. Another case involved a Texas trooper killed in cold blood while approaching the driver of a vehicle with a defective headlight. The driver attempted a temporary insanity defense based on the claim he felt hypnotized by songs on a 2 Pac [Shakur] album, that the anti-police lyrics "took control, devouring [him] like an animal, compelling his subconscious mind to kill the approaching trooper." Two of the nation's leading psychiatrists were called as expert witnesses in support of this failed defense.

Social Morality

It has become prevalent, especially among the slacker generations, Generation X and Generation 13, to join the old World War II generation in self-righteous, totally gratuitous Sixties-bashing, as if all our social problems, especially our declining social morality, started with the free-for-all, "any thing goes" hippie movement of the 1960s. This time period is often blamed for giving birth to rising hedonism, the questioning of authority, unbridled pursuit of pleasure, the abandonment of family responsibility, demand for illicit drugs, and a number of other social ills. Sometimes, even the AIDS epidemic is blamed on the 1960s, although such accusers are off by about two decades.

To sixties-bashers, today's juvenile "super predators" are

nothing but a long line of troubled youngsters who have grown up in more extreme conditions of declining social morality than the generation before them. Their thinking is that each generation since the sixties has tried hard to outdo one another in expressing the attitude that "nothing really matters," culminating in the present teenage regard for angst and irony so common in contemporary culture.

I remember the sixties, with all its collective violence, drug-crazed looniness, challenges to authority, and more social causes than you could possibly join in on. Maybe I'm biased, but I just don't see a connection between the idealism and cynicism of that period and the vacant, stone-cold, remorseless irony of today's juvenile offenders. In fact, I wish today's generations had more idealism and cynicism, but I understand that as a whole, they are facing some difficult challenges. They grew up with nothing but sound bites instead of reasoned discourse about social problems, they learned from AIDS that sex kills and you should always use a condom, they got MTV and syndicated talk shows as entertainment fodder, they continue to be exploited in low-paying McJobs and are told that this service sector is the fastest growing part of the economy, they are told that Social Security will probably not be there for them, and they are the first generation in American history to probably do worse economically than their parents.

"Violence is not a game; it's not fun; it's not something that we do for entertainment. Violence kills and maims."

Violence in the Media Contributes to Juvenile Crime

Dave Grossman

Many experts claim that recent incidents of violent crime are directly related to the amount of violence found in movies, news broadcasts, and video games. Children, especially in single-parent homes, often spend more time watching television than with their families and grow up with television heroes as their role models. In the following viewpoint, Dave Grossman makes this argument, contending that the representation of violent murders on television often stimulates what he calls "cluster murders," in which children reenact the violence they see on the screen. Dave Grossman is an expert on the psychology of killing and is the author of *On Killing* and the co-author of *Stop Teaching Our Kids to Kill.*

As you read, consider the following questions:
1. What, according to the author, is a "copycat" suicide?
2. What are two unsuccessful solutions to violence in the media, according to Grossman?
3. What are three suggestions the author offers to changing American culture?

Excerpted from Dave Grossman, "We Are Training Our Kids to Kill," *Saturday Evening Post*, September/October 1999. Reprinted by permission of the author.

Today, the media are providing our children with many, perhaps most, of their role models. Kids like to emulate their role models. Tragically, media-inspired copycat crimes are now a fact of life. This is the part of juvenile crime reporting that the TV networks would rather not talk about.

Research in the 1970s demonstrated the existence of "cluster suicides" in which the local TV reporting of teen suicides directly caused numerous copycat suicides by impressionable teenagers. Somewhere in every population there are potentially suicidal kids who will say to themselves, "Well, I'll show all those people who have been mean to me. Then I'll get my picture on TV, too."

Because of this research, television stations today generally do not cover suicides. But when the pictures of teenage killers appear on TV, the effect is the same. Somewhere there is a potentially violent boy who says to himself, "Well, I'll shoot all those people who have been mean to me. Then I'll get my picture on TV, too."

Thus we get copycat cluster murders that work their way across America like a virus spread by the six o'clock news. No matter what someone has done, if you put his picture on TV, you have made him a celebrity, and someone somewhere will want to emulate him.

The Influence of Role Models

The lineage of the Jonesboro shootings [where two boys, eleven and thirteen, killed four girls and a teacher in March 1998] began at Pearl, Mississippi, fewer than four months before. In Pearl, a 16-year-old boy was accused of killing his mother and then going to his school and shooting nine students, two of whom died, including his ex-girlfriend. Two months later, this virus spread to Paducah, Kentucky, where a 14-year-old boy was arrested for killing three students and wounding five others.

A very important step in the spread of this copycat crime virus occurred in Stamps, Arkansas, 15 days after Pearl and just a little over 90 days before Jonesboro. In Stamps, a 14-year-old boy who was angry with his schoolmates hid in the woods and fired at children as they came out of school. Sound familiar? Only two children were injured in this crime, so most of the world didn't hear about it; but it got great regional coverage on TV, and two little boys in Jonesboro, Arkansas, probably did hear about it.

And then there was Springfield, Oregon, on May 21, 1998, and so many others. Is this a reasonable price to pay for the TV networks' "right" to turn juvenile defendants into celebrities and role models by playing up their pictures on TV?

Our society needs to be informed about these crimes, but when the images of the young killers are broadcast on television, they become role models. The average preschooler in America watches 27 hours of television a week. The average child gets more one-on-one communication from TV than from all her parents and teachers combined. The ultimate achievement for our children is to get their picture on TV. The solution is simple, and it comes straight out of the sociology literature: The media have every right and responsibility to tell the story, but they must be persuaded not to glorify the killers by presenting their images on TV.

Unlearning Violence

What is the road home from the dark and lonely place to which we have traveled? One route infringes on civil liberties. The city of New York has made remarkable progress in recent years in bringing down crime rates, but they may have done so at the expense of some civil liberties. People who are fearful say that is a price they are willing to pay.

Another route would be to "just turn it off." If you don't like what is on television, use the "off" button. Yet, if all the parents of the 15 shooting victims in Jonesboro had protected their children from TV violence, it wouldn't have done a bit of good because somewhere there were two little boys whose parents didn't "just turn it off."

Another route to reduced violence is gun control. I don't want to downplay that option, but America is trapped in a vicious cycle when we talk about gun control. Americans don't trust the government. Most believe that each of us should be responsible for taking care of our families and ourselves. That's one of our great strengths—but it is also a great weakness. When the media foster fear and perpetuate a milieu of violence, Americans arm themselves in order to deal with that violence. And the more guns there are out there, the more violence there is. And the more violence there is, the greater the desire for guns.

We are trapped in this spiral of self-reliance and lack of trust. Real progress will never be made until we reduce this level of fear. As a historian, I tell you it will take decades—maybe even a century—before we wean Americans off their guns. Until we reduce the fear of violent crime, many Americans would sooner "die" than give up their guns.

Fighting Back

We need to make progress in the fight against child abuse, racism, and poverty, and in rebuilding our families. No one is denying that the breakdown of the family is a factor. But nations without our divorce rate are also having increases in violence. Research demonstrates that one major source of harm associated with single-parent families occurs when the TV becomes both the nanny and the second parent.

Gary Varvel. Reprinted with permission.

Work is needed in all these areas, but there is a new front—taking on the producers and purveyors of media violence. Simply put, we ought to work toward legislation that outlaws violent video games for children. There is no constitutional right for a child to play an interactive video game that teaches him weapons-handling skills or that simulates destruction of God's creatures.

The day may also be coming when we are able to seat juries in America who are willing to sock it to the networks and video game promoters in the only place they'll really feel it—their wallets. After the Jonesboro shootings, *Time* magazine said, "As for media violence, the debate there is fast approaching the same point that discussions about the health impact of tobacco reached some time ago—it's over. Few researchers bother any longer to dispute that bloodshed on TV and in the movies has an effect on kids who witness it" (April 6, 1998).

Most of all, the American people need to learn the lesson of Jonesboro. Violence is not a game; it's not fun; it's not something that we do for entertainment. Violence kills and maims.

Every parent in America needs to be warned of the impact that TV and other forms of violent media have on their children, just as we would warn them of some widespread carcinogen. The problem is that the TV networks, which use the public airwaves we have licensed to them, are our key means of public education in America. And they are stonewalling.

In the days after the Jonesboro shootings, I was interviewed on Canadian national TV, the British Broadcasting Company, and many U.S. and international radio shows and newspapers. But the American television networks simply would not touch this aspect of the story. Never in my experience as a historian and a psychologist have I seen any institution in America so clearly responsible for so very many deaths and so clearly abusing their publicly licensed authority and power to cover up their guilt. . . .

Alternatives to Television

A CBS executive once told me his child-rearing plan. He knows all about the link between television and violence. His own in-house people have advised him to protect his child from the poison his industry is bringing to America's children. He is not going to expose his child to TV until she's old enough to learn how to read. And then he will select very carefully what she sees. He and his wife plan to send her to a day-care center that has no television, and he plans to show her only age-appropriate videos.

Responsible Parenting

Parents should know that the impact on children of television, movies, music, video games, and the Internet arises not only form the kinds of behavior they promote, but also from the other activities they replace. A Canadian study analyzed the changes in how families living in a small town spent their days before and after television was introduced. The study found that after television became available, people spent less time talking, socializing outside the home, doing household tasks, engaging in leisure activities, and being involved in community activities. People even slept less once the television entered the home. The lesson: Parents should supply their children with alternatives to television, movies, music, video games, and the Internet. Regularly providing things such as art supplies, books to read, athletic activities, or outdoor excursions will reduce the number of arguments about what to watch on television and teach children how to enjoy a broader range of activities.

Parents should realize that there is simply no substitute for close adult supervision of, and involvement in, the lives of their children. Parents must take time to learn what their children are viewing and playing. Even the most seemingly trivial supervision can have a profound effect. For instance, many school and public libraries have found that simply placing computers in conspicuous public view deters children from inappropriate use. Reducing the effects of media violence requires sound parenting as well as responsible, responsive government.

Orrin G. Hatch, "Children, Violence, and the Media: A Report for Parents and Policymakers," September 14, 1999.

That should be the bare minimum with children: Show them only age-appropriate videos and think hard about what is age appropriate. . . .

There are many other things that we can do to help change our culture. Youth activities can provide alternatives to television, and churches can lead the way in providing alternative locations for latchkey children. Fellowship groups can provide guidance and support to young parents as they strive to raise their children without the destructive influences of the media. Mentoring programs can pair mature, educated adults with young parents to help them through the preschool ages without using the TV as a baby-sitter. And most of all, the churches can provide the clarion call of decency and love and peace as an alternative to death and destruction—not just for the sake of the church, but for the transformation of our culture.

*"No direct, causal link between exposure to
mock violence in the media and subsequent
violent behavior has ever been
demonstrated."*

Violence in the Media Does Not Contribute to Juvenile Crime

Richard Rhodes

Entertainment has always been targeted as a cause of youth
violence, from the novels of Mark Twain in the 1800s to today's Doom, a popular video game. Proponents claim that
not only do juveniles reenact what they see on the television
screen and the Internet, but they also become desensitized
to graphic portrayals of brutality. Opponents argue that
there is no direct correlation between artificial violence in
the media and the violence committed by juveniles. In the
following viewpoint, Richard Rhodes makes this argument.
He claims that juveniles learn violent behavior from abusive
family members or peers, not from cartoons or movies.
Richard Rhodes is a self-described amateur criminologist
and the author of *Why They Kill: The Discoveries of a Maverick Criminologist.*

As you read, consider the following questions:
1. According to the author, to what do historians attribute
   the decline in private violence?
2. What does the British scholar Martin Barker find odd
   about the theory of desensitization?
3. Where does the author believe children learn violent
   behavior?

Excerpted from Richard Rhodes, "Hollow Claims About Fantasy Violence," *The
New York Times*, September 17, 2000. Copyright © 2000 by The New York Times
Company. Reprinted with permission.

Is there really a link between entertainment and violent behavior?

The American Medical Association, the American Psychological Association, the American Academy of Pediatrics and the National Institute of Mental Health all say yes. They base their claims on social science research that has been sharply criticized and disputed within the social science profession, especially outside the United States. In fact, no direct, causal link between exposure to mock violence in the media and subsequent violent behavior has ever been demonstrated, and the few claims of modest correlation have been contradicted by other findings, sometimes in the same studies.

History alone should call such a link into question. Private violence has been declining in the West since the media-barren late Middle Ages, when homicide rates are estimated to have been 10 times what they are in Western nations today. Historians attribute the decline to improving social controls over violence—police forces and common access to courts of law—and to a shift away from brutal physical punishment in child-rearing (a practice that still appears as a common factor in the background of violent criminals today).

Foreign Comparisons

The American Medical Association has based its endorsement of the media violence theory in major part on the studies of Brandon Centerwall, a psychiatrist in Seattle. Dr. Centerwall compared the murder rates for whites in three countries from 1945 to 1974 with numbers for television set ownership. Until 1975, television broadcasting was banned in South Africa, and "white homicide rates remained stable" there, Dr. Centerwall found, while corresponding rates in Canada and the United States doubled after television was introduced. A spectacular finding, but it is meaningless. As Franklin E. Zimring and Gordon Hawkins of the University of California at Berkeley subsequently pointed out, homicide rates in France, Germany, Italy and Japan either failed to change with increasing television ownership in the same period or actually declined, and American homicide rates have more recently been sharply declining despite a proliferation of popular media outlets—not only movies and television, but also video games and the Internet.

Other social science that supposedly undergirds the theory, too, is marginal and problematic. Laboratory studies that expose children to selected incidents of televised mock violence and then assess changes in the children's behavior have sometimes found more "aggressive" behavior after the exposure—usually verbal, occasionally physical.

Violent Tragedies Are Rare

Logic dictates that, if movies, television, video games, and the Internet are responsible for [violent] behavior, then why is [the tragedy in Littleton] so unusual? If these media so corrupt the minds and hearts and souls of America's young people, then why doesn't this kind of activity happen every day? Why is the event itself so bizarre, so unfamiliar that it grabs the headlines of news media around the world? . . .

Blaming the now popular forms of media for creating these damaged, pathetic human beings [Dylan Klebold and Eric Harris] only clouds the issue and creates the kind of censorship which in the past has watered down and destroyed our forms of communication.

Joe Saltzman, *USA Today*, July 29, 1999.

But sometimes the control group, shown incidents judged not to be violent, behaves more aggressively afterward than the test group; sometimes comedy produces the more aggressive behavior; and sometimes there's no change. The only obvious conclusion is that sitting and watching television stimulates subsequent physical activity. Any kid could tell you that.

As for those who claim that entertainment promotes violent behavior by desensitizing people to violence, the British scholar Martin Barker offers this critique: "Their claim is that the materials they judge to be harmful can only influence us by trying to make us be the same as them. So horrible things will make us horrible—not horrified. Terrifying things will make us terrifying—not terrified. To see something aggressive makes us feel aggressive—not aggressed against. This idea is so odd, it is hard to know where to begin in challenging it."

Even more influential on national policy has been a 22-

year study by two University of Michigan psychologists, Leonard D. Eron and L. Rowell Huesmann, of boys exposed to so-called violent media. The Telecommunications Act of 1996, which mandated the television V-chip, allowing parents to screen out unwanted programming, invoked these findings, asserting, "Studies have shown that children exposed to violent video programming at a young age have a higher tendency for violent and aggressive behavior later in life than children not so exposed."

Well, not exactly. Following 875 children in upstate New York from third grade through high school, the psychologists found a correlation between a preference for violent television at age 8 and aggressiveness at age 18. The correlation—0.31—would mean television accounted for about 10 percent of the influences that led to this behavior. But the correlation only turned up in one of three measures of aggression: the assessment of students by their peers. It didn't show up in students' reports about themselves or in psychological testing. And for girls, there was no correlation at all.

The Reality of Child Abuse

Despite the lack of evidence, politicians can't resist blaming the media for violence. They can stake out the moral high ground confident that the First Amendment will protect them from having to actually write legislation that would be likely to alienate the entertainment industry. Some use the issue as a smoke screen to avoid having to confront gun control.

But violence isn't learned from mock violence. There is good evidence—causal evidence, not correlational—that it's learned in personal violent encounters, beginning with the brutalization of children by their parents or their peers.

The money spent on all the social science research I've described was diverted from the National Institute of Mental Health budget by reducing support for the construction of community mental health centers. To this day there is no standardized reporting system for emergency-room findings of physical child abuse. Violence is on the decline in America, but if we want to reduce it even further, protecting children from real violence in their real lives—not the pale shadow of mock violence—is the place to begin.

*"Once their rage is stoked and justified, . . .
[kids] can grab a handy semiautomatic
and, borrowing cool moves from the latest
mayhem flick, go blow away their
classmates."*

Guns Contribute to Juvenile Crime

Bob Levin

On April 20, 1999, in Littleton, Colorado, two students, Eric
Harris and Dylan Klebold, killed thirteen and wounded
twenty-one at Columbine High School using two shotguns, a
rifle, and a nine-millimeter pistol. While many argue that the
boys would have found some other way to harm the students
they resented, others argue that the tragedy could not have
occurred without the ready access they had to guns. In the following viewpoint, Bob Levin makes this argument, claiming
that although the Second Amendment protects America's
right to bear arms, it also puts dangerous weapons in the
hands of immature, confused teenagers. Levin is a contributing editor at *Maclean's*, a weekly Canadian newsmagazine.

As you read, consider the following questions:
1. Where does the author feel that the National Rifle
   Association (NRA) goes wrong?
2. What does Levin give as three examples of the "gun
   culture"?
3. According to Levin, what is the potent combination of
   societal dysfunction portrayed in the film *Rebel Without
   a Cause*?

Reprinted, with permission, from Bob Levin, "Casualties of the Right to Bear
Arms," *Maclean's*, May 3, 1999.

OK, let's get this straight. The kids [Dylan Klebold and Eric Harris]—the killers—called themselves the Trenchcoat Mafia. They were into heavy-metal music, violent video games, black lipstick and nail polish; they sewed swastikas on their black dusters and talked about Hitler, about how to buy Uzis and build pipe bombs. But they were just loners, outcasts. Geeks. A little weird. Kids other kids made fun of. They didn't seem to be a problem.

What's wrong with this picture?

We go looking for answers, we always do, knowing full well there may be none. A couple of disturbed kids—it could happen anywhere, any time, it doesn't mean anything. Maybe it's easier to think that. Otherwise you have to dissect the whole culture, to blame, as American conservatives do, the permissive society, or, taking the liberal line, to blame guns. You have to consider negligent parents and oblivious educators and whether you really need that pistol in the drawer, and you have to wonder what's going on—how benumbed we've all become—when kids who give the Nazi salute after rolling strikes in the school bowling league are just different, not a problem.

Maybe, in a way, the conservatives and liberals are both right. Sure, there have always been outcast kids, but today's outcasts can descend into [the video game] Doom or the [World Wrestling Federation] (WWF) or [the music of] Marilyn Manson, they can commune with like-minded losers on Internet hate sites and not feel so alone. And once their rage is stoked and justified, once they're deep into the darkness and set to let loose as kids have long done in fast cars or on bad drugs or simply with a clothesline in a closet, they can grab a handy semiautomatic and, borrowing cool moves from the latest mayhem flick, go blow away their classmates.

The Gun Culture

That this [massacre] happened in Littleton, Colo.—so serene and scrub-faced it ought to be in Canada—is evidence enough that no place is immune. But you can't shoot people without a gun and this is where the conservatives and the odious National Rifle Association (NRA) go so unconscionably wrong, spouting their endless Second Amendment drivel about the right to bear arms, quoting [Thomas] Jefferson and [James] Madison and [Alexander] Hamilton on the importance of a well-girded citizenry, as if the enemy were still a colonial power threatening American liberty at musket-point and not drive-by shooters and trigger-happy teens. 'I'm the NRA,' goes the slogan, and a nation of 270 million people bristles with some 230 million guns (compared with seven million among 30 million Canadians). Every year, guns kill 13.7 Americans per 100,000 (about 3.8 Canadians per 100,000); in 1996–1997, more than 6,000 U.S. students were expelled for packing heat to school.

"WELL, IF ALL THE OTHER KIDS HAD GUNS, THEY COULD HAVE PROTECTED THEMSELVES"

© 1999 Herblock at *The Washington Post*. Reprinted with permission.

The gun culture: you can't overemphasize how ubiquitous it is. I grew up in the States and it still strikes me. In Indiana a divorced woman I knew slept with a loaded handgun under her pillow, ready for any intruder; the kid in the apartment below me got drunk one night and shot up the fire station; a stroll in the country ended with a woman popping up from behind my car and poking me in the gut with a shotgun, grilling me on why I'd walked on her property. (Her husband, pedalling up with his rifle lying conveniently across his handlebars, was a friendlier sort.) In Oklahoma, dinner at a new acquaintance's house closed with the kids— a grade-school boy and girl—going out 'to do some shooting' and I assumed hoops until I heard the gunfire. In Atlanta, where most whites live north of I-20 and blacks south of it, my wife was officially told, upon starting work at the newspaper downtown, that while many people bring guns to the office please check them at the front desk before riding up to the newsroom.

America's Precious Freedoms

This is a national obsession and it's lunacy. On the NRA's Web site, its president Charlton Heston—who likes to point out that in the movies he played three presidents, several kings, a few saints, Old and New Testament prophets and of course Moses—informs members (and you can hear that voice) that the schedule of the 1999 national meeting in Denver has been modified 'to show our profound sympathy and respect for the families and communities . . . in their time of great loss.'

Which is a delicate way of saying that, politically speaking, this is not the best moment for gaudy bazaars of enough advanced weaponry to invade Yugoslavia, but neither, apparently, is it a time to reconsider their insistence on preserving 'our precious freedoms' in the hopes of maybe saving a few kids.

Guns, a death-obsessed culture, disaffected youths: it's a potent combination but it's hardly new. In 1955, James Dean, Natalie Wood and Sal Mineo were the troubled teens in *Rebel Without a Cause*, playing out their alienation with knives, guns and killer hot rods. 'Teenage terror torn from today's headlines,' blared the movie poster and adults were appalled, saying the film advocated violence, madness and death and unfairly indicted parents.

We look for answers, always, and maybe sometimes the answers are too simplistic. Maybe you can't blame Littleton on Doom and heavy metal. Maybe the whole safety issue is overstated, blown up by a few horrific incidents. The U.S. Centers for Disease Control and Prevention says fewer than one per cent of all homicides among school-age children occur in or around schools, which sounds almost reassuring. But don't try that one on the parents of 14 Colorado kids whose rights to life, liberty and the pursuit of happiness were snuffed out by the right to bear arms.

"Generations of American youths have grown up around guns without feeling at all compelled to commit multiple murder."

Guns Do Not Contribute to Juvenile Crime

Timothy Wheeler

The recent incidents of school shootings have sparked debates over the accessibility of guns to minors. Opponents argue that juveniles could not commit such mass murders as the Springfield, Oregon, shooting, in which Kip Kinkel murdered two and wounded twenty in 1998, without having such ready access to guns. Proponents of gun ownership, however, argue that guns have been a part of American culture for centuries without juveniles using them on their classmates. In the following viewpoint, Timothy Wheeler makes this argument, claiming that individuals are to blame for violence, not guns. Wheeler is the director of Doctors for Responsible Gun Ownership, a project of the Claremont Institute that supports the safe and lawful use of firearms.

As you read, consider the following questions:
1. Why does the author claim that guns do not cause juvenile violence?
2. What does the author offer as a popular explanation of criminal behavior other than guns?
3. Why do the commonly offered explanations for youth violence fail, according to Wheeler?

Reprinted, with permission, from Timothy Wheeler, "Blaming the Guns," *The Washington Times*, June 2, 1998.

In Springfield, Oregon this past week [1998] fifteen year-old Kip Kinkel was arraigned in court, charged with murdering two classmates and wounding twenty others in a cafeteria shooting rampage. It appears likely that the young man had murdered his parents as well.

This is the latest in a string of a half dozen similar nightmares that have taken place across the nation during the 1997-98 school year, including Edinboro, Pennsylvania; Jonesboro, Arkansas; West Paducah, Kentucky; and Pearl, Mississippi. All involved young killers with guns and without self-restraint. Nearly everyone agrees that we have moved beyond the realm of mere coincidence, that there is some connection between these horrible events. But that's where the agreement ends.

As parents grieved last month in Jonesboro, television commentator Katie Couric suggested that the shootings were rooted in a gun and hunting culture. She was not alone in this, and it's easy to see why. Each of this year's tragedies took place in regions where legal gun ownership is commonplace, and where youngsters are often taught about firearms.

But if the blame lay solely with "gun culture," one should expect this sort of violence to have happened all along in American history. Generations of American youths have grown up around guns without feeling at all compelled to commit multiple murder. To the contrary, most young people who train today in the shooting sports learn excellence and discipline as they do in any sport. Kim Rhode of El Monte, California, has practiced with firearms since she was in grade school. If guns really do cause violence, Kim should be in serious trouble with the law by now. Instead, at seventeen she became the youngest woman in Olympic history to win a gold medal in a shooting sport.

If guns themselves don't cause criminal behavior, another popular explanation is the long-term effects of violent television, movies, and video games. In his May 23 radio address, President Clinton said the recent shootings are "symptoms of a changing culture that desensitizes our children to violence, where most teenagers have seen hundreds or even thousands of murders on television and in movies and in video games before they graduate from high school, where too many young people seem unable or unwilling to take responsibility for their actions, and where all too often everyday conflicts are resolved not with words but with weapons, which, even when illegal to possess by children, are all too easy to get."

But however debased our popular culture might have become—and debased it certainly is —this explanation is as unsatisfying as the first: Only a tiny fraction of the millions of children exposed to TV violence go on to imitate the mayhem they have seen portrayed by Hollywood actors.

Guns Save Lives

America may be obsessed with guns, but much of what passes as fact simply isn't true. The news media focus on tragic outcomes, while ignoring tragic events that were avoided. Rarely do we hear about the more than two million times each year that people use guns defensively—including cases in which public shootings are stopped before they happen. Dramatic stories of mothers using guns to prevent their children from being kidnapped by car-jackers seldom even make the local news.

John R. Lott, *Wall Street Journal*, November 11, 1998.

Both explanations fail because they try to pin the blame for violence on something outside the individual—they deny that a young man is ultimately responsible for his own actions. Blaming anything or anyone but the perpetrator himself has become the order of the day. Perhaps the most extreme example of this was the infamous "twinkie defense" employed by the murderer of San Francisco Mayor Moscone. The accused could not be held responsible, his attorney argued, because he had consumed junk food. Since that trial we have grown used to hearing that every action, good or evil, is not based on free will, but is the result of some exterior cause, whether too much TV, a bad family life, or access to a weapon. This is the result of a long-term philosophical shift away from the idea of human free will, and the results of that shift have now come home to roost with the children of the baby boom generation.

The good news is that we are finally recognizing the terrible consequences of this philosophy, as we see firsthand the results of a generation of moral neglect of our young people. Appalled by the lack of standards in public schools, parents are increasingly placing their children in private academies or church-sponsored schools where responsibility and morality can legally be taught. Some small colleges are quietly pursuing curricula which pay homage to the classics, politically correct or not. It took us a generation to trash the truth, and we will struggle just as long in coming to our moral senses as a nation.

In the meantime we can pass a law to ban more guns, or place new ratings codes on TV, movies, and video games. But the former will only serve to redefine as criminals millions of previously law-abiding citizens, and the latter will do nothing to change what consumers want to buy. What law can remedy fatal character defects? By banning the culture of guns and hunting we will not stop teen murderers. But by rebuilding a culture of loving, moral guidance for our children we will.

"Poverty is so strongly connected to nearly everything adults think is wrong with 'kids today'. . . that it dwarfs ever other factor."

The Root Cause of Juvenile Crime and Violence Is Poverty

Mike Males

Many factors are blamed for the problem of juvenile crime and violence, such as violence on television and video games, the breakdown of the family, or a decline in religious values. In the following viewpoint, Mike Males argues that most violent juvenile crime occurs in communities where the average income is below the United States poverty level. He claims that children living in poverty-stricken areas suffer higher gun fatality rates than more affluent children and that children of color are more often killed than white children. He contends that more effort should be put into reducing poverty than punishing criminals. Males is a senior researcher with the Center on Juvenile and Criminal Justice and a sociology instructor at the University of California, Santa Cruz.

As you read, consider the following questions:
1. What, according to Males, do New Democrats and Republicans agree are "today's big menaces to kids"?
2. What does Males claim was the crucial factor no one mentioned when crime tripled in the late 1980s and early 1990s?
3. What is California's fastest growing felon and prison population, according to the author?

Reprinted, with permission, from Mike Males, "Leave the Kids Alone: Poverty Is Their Real Problem," *In These Times*, June 12, 2000.

In a boom economy, the most recent figures show that a staggering 40 percent of America's children and youth remain in low-income families. Thirteen million are poor, and 6 million of those suffer destitution in households with less than half of poverty-level income. U.S. child poverty rates are two to 10 times higher than in Western Europe, Canada or Australia. Poverty is so strongly connected to nearly everything adults think is wrong with "kids today"—murder, violent crime, unintended pregnancy, AIDS, smoking, dropping out of school—that it dwarfs every other factor.

Yet child poverty is rarely discussed today, buried under the popular, all-consuming "values" crusade and by the usefulness of children in pushing other agendas. New Democrats and Republicans agree that today's big menaces to kids are violent video games, TV, caffeine, R-rated movies, unfiltered Internet porn, raves, gangstas, Marilyn Manson, baggy pants, or any unmonitored free time. White kids with guns grace "kids without a conscience" cover stories in *People* and *Rolling Stone* that dismiss poverty as irrelevant.

Poverty and Gun Fatality Rates

But in the real world, the likelihood of a youth being killed by gunfire, getting arrested, going to prison or dying before age 25 has a lot more to do with how poor he or she is. Obsession with fictional screen images crowds out realities of grinding poverty, crumbling schools, vanished jobs and grownups in disarray. Culture warriors such as President Bill Clinton, former Education Secretary Bill Bennett, the Manhattan Institute's Kay Hymowitz, *Tribe Apart* author Patricia Hersch and West Point video-game blamer Dave Grossman cite (or more often distort) scary statistics to buttress claims of a "youth culture" driven by pop-culture corruption into mass degeneration.

In truth, where U.S. kids enjoy low poverty rates like those of Europe, there are correspondingly low murder and gun-fatality rates. In California's five richest urban counties, with a combined population of 6 million, white teen-agers' poverty rates average 4 percent—similar to those of Scandinavian youth. Even in this state [California] with one of America's highest gun-fatality rates—where white households are the most likely to harbor guns, violent cable channels and video games—the gun death rate among white teens (three per 100,000) is as low as Sweden's or Canada's. Meanwhile, poorer California youth of all colors (the vast majority black, Latino and Asian) suffer gun-fatality rates three to eight times higher. Poverty is associated with 85 percent of gun deaths among children and youths, as well as the adults who commit most murders of children. The figures on gun murders per 100,000 youths show that class, not race, is the issue: richer white (0.8), middle-income white (2.1), lower-income color (3.1), poorer color (6.7). (Poorer California white youth are more affluent than the average youth of color.)

Statistics Exclude the Affluent

During the late '80s and early '90s, when the press, police and politicians went hysterical over the tripling in juvenile firearms homicides, no one mentioned a crucial factor clearly visible in crime statistics in major states like California, New York and Pennsylvania. There was no increase in murder among America's middle-class and affluent youths, whose trends stayed at low levels throughout the period. In fact, among California's white teen-agers, murder rates have dropped 40 percent over the past 25 years (especially during the '90s, when violent video games and movies supposedly were inciting them).

While upscale, suburban kids occasionally committed mayhem, the high rates of teenage murder and gun fatality in the early '90s occurred only among poorer youths, overwhelmingly those of color—especially youths caught in or between gangs warring to supply the soaring drug demands of white suburban adults.

So, if poverty is tied to higher risks of violence, and if more kids are poorer today, is the intense fear of "youth violence" exploited by politicians such as President Clinton and former California Governor Pete Wilson justified?

No. For even as quotable crime authorities like Northeastern University's James Alan Fox and Princeton's John Dilulio warned in the mid-'90s that a new breed of "godless, fatherless, jobless . . . adolescent superpredators" would bring a "bloodbath," California youth were displaying dramatic decreases in crime. By the late '90s, as school shootings brought renewed cries that "killer white kids" had joined ghetto superpredators in a nationwide teen-murder epidemic, California teen-agers of all colors displayed their lowest rate of murder and serious crime in three decades.

Getting Tough Is Not a Solution

It would stand to reason that if poverty were reduced, the rate of violent crime would also be reduced. But that option is deemed unworkable and too expensive by the conservatives. Better to hire more police, build more prisons and impose longer prison sentences at younger ages. Unfortunately, getting tough doesn't work. States such as California, Texas and Oklahoma have tried all of these remedies and all three states have seen record increases in violent crime.

Drugs, easy access to guns and a violent popular culture are all contributing factors to this nation's high rate of violent crime. This cannot be denied. But when one gets down to the nut, poverty remains the biggest factor of them all. But it is politically easier to scapegoat teens than to do something about the alarming number of American kids that are growing up in poverty.

Randolph T. Holhut, *The Written Word*, 1996.

Yet predictions of teen-age apocalypse became the excuse for a virulent, anti-youth reaction among affluent white voters and politicians. This led to massive defunding of California's once-proud school and university system, corporate abandonment of the inner-city, abolition of youth services and massive prison expansion. Left and right disagreed on what instigated the "youth crisis" and what should be done, but everyone battened the hatches.

Growing Up Too Fast

Instead, California's new millennium was greeted by a youth population less likely to abuse drugs and alcohol, less suicidal, less likely to die in traffic wrecks, more law-abiding, more likely to graduate from high school and enter college, and more apt to be employed and involved in community volunteerism than any generation in decades. From the mid-

'70s to the late '90s, California's rates of youth suicides, violent deaths and felony arrests dropped 40 to 60 percent, and drug-related deaths fell an astounding 90 percent. These improvements predated the current fervor for cracking down on kids, and remain strongest in areas such as San Francisco, where get-tough curfews, drug enforcement and prosecution of youths as adults were rejected by authorities.

Superficially, the fact that kids are getting poorer and better might seem to excuse Washington's current proclivities, but closer analysis reveals that widespread poverty and packed schools are serious barriers to this generation. Youth behavior improved because it had to. Explosions in drug abuse, crime and family disarray among Baby Boomers, and the War on Drugs' punitive strategies produced a startling crisis: California's fastest-growing felon and prison population by far is white adults 30 and older, followed by adults of color. Deteriorating adult behavior forced millions of youths to assume adult responsibilities earlier in life—a precocity, ironically, greeted with cultural warriors' misplaced horror that media-savvy kids "are growing up too fast."

Poverty, narrowed opportunity and harsher anti-crime policies are not the causes of improved youth behavior; they remain impediments reflected in struggles with chaotic families, crowded schools, massive student debt, race- and class-based inequality, and dead-end jobs. Even though young people have improved as a generation due to their own efforts and a few good programs, poverty's effects still are seen in poorer populations' sharply higher crime and violent death statistics.

It is long past time for liberal groups concerned with murder and firearms deaths to make reducing poverty their priority. America's high rates of child and youth poverty are not simply evidence of preventable inequality, but preventable fatality.

"For all the talk about the complexities of the 'root causes' of crime, there is one root cause which overwhelms all the rest: fatherlessness."

The Root Cause of Juvenile Crime and Violence Is Fatherlessness

Dave Kopel

While experts argue about the causes of juvenile crime and violence, citing a decline in morality, poverty, or television violence, statistics show that the divorce rate is currently up to 50 percent, and that an increasing number of children are being raised without fathers. In the following viewpoint, Dave Kopel argues that this epidemic of fatherlessness is the major cause of juvenile crime and violence because children lacking adult male authority figures are more likely to commit crimes. He contends that until the problem of illegitimate children is solved, crime control will remain ineffective. Kopel is a property lawyer in Los Angeles and a contributing columnist for the *National Review*, a conservative journal of opinion.

As you read, consider the following questions:
1. What does the juvenile detention counselor quoted by the author think does not exist?
2. What social and economic variables does the author claim have not changed since 1960?
3. How have welfare policies helped spur the rise in illegitimacy, according to the author?

Reprinted, with permission, from Dave Kopel, "Fatherlessness: The Root Cause," *National Review Online*, May 2, 2000; © 2000 by National Review, Inc., National Review Online, www.nationalreview.com.

The continuing rise in illegitimacy rates is terrible news not just for the children themselves, but for every potential crime victim in America. For all the talk about the complexities of the "root causes" of crime, there is one root cause which overwhelms all the rest: fatherlessness.

As Pat Moynihan wrote in 1965: "From the wild Irish slums of the nineteenth-century Eastern seaboard to the riot-torn suburbs of Los Angeles, there is one unmistakable lesson in American history: A community that allows a large number of young men to grow up in broken families, dominated by women, never acquiring a stable relationship to male authority, never acquiring any rational expectations about the future—that community asks for and gets chaos. . . . [In such a society] crime, violence, unrest, unrestrained [rebellion against] whole social structure—these are not only to be expected, they are virtually inevitable."

Statistical Evidence

A Detroit study found that about 70 percent of juvenile homicide perpetrators did not live with both parents. Another study found that of girls committed to the California Youth Authority (for serious delinquents), 93 percent came from non-intact homes. Nationally, seventy percent of youths incarcerated in state reform institutions come from single-parent or no-parent homes. A survey of juvenile delinquents in state custody in Wisconsin found that fewer than 1/6 came from intact families; over two-fifths were illegitimate.

Said one counselor at a juvenile detention facility in California: "You find a gang member who comes from a complete nuclear family, a kid who has never been exposed [to] any kind of abuse, I'd like to meet him . . . a real gangbanger who comes from a happy, balanced home, who's got a good opinion himself. I don't think that kid exists."

Young black males from single-parent families are twice as likely to engage in crime as young black males from two-parent families. If the single-parent family is in a neighborhood with a large number of other single-parent families, the odds of the young man becoming involved in crime are tripled. These findings are based on a study conducted for the Department of Health and Human Services by M. Anne Hill and June O'Neill of Baruch College. The study held constant all socioeconomic variables (such as income, parental education, or urban setting) other than single parenthood.

Analysis of Single-Parent Families

Unless current trends change, by 2010 over half of all children born in the United States will be born to unmarried women and will be raised with no father. According to Surgeon General Jocelyn Elders—and according to 20% of white teenagers, 30% of Hispanic teenagers, and 40% of Black teenagers—unmarried parenthood is simply another lifestyle choice. It is not. . . . It is a death style. It is the most important single cause of the collapse of American society. . . .

Children from single-parent families are 40 to 75% more likely to repeat a grade in school, and 70% more likely to be expelled from school than children from a two-parent home. The poverty rate for families headed by a single mother is seven times higher than the rate for two-parent households. . . . Single-parent families usually are poorer. About half the difference in income inequality (the gap between rich and poor) between 1969 and 1989 was due to the sharply increasing number of single-parent families.

Being raised in a single-parent family significantly increases the prospects that the child will have a troubled family life when she grows up. A white woman who grows up in a single-parent family is 164% more likely to have an illegitimate child; 111% more likely to bear a child while she is still a teenager; and (if she eventually does marry) 92% more likely to get divorced.

Dave Kopel, Andrew Kelly, Tim Garret, Greg Bledsoe, and Ben Kwitek,
"Independence Institute: Independence Issue Paper," 1999.

Crime has often been thought to be a problem of race or poverty, since poor people and racial minorities comprise a larger portion of the violent criminal population than of the population as a whole. But in fact, the causal link between fatherlessness and crime "is so strong that controlling for family configuration erases the relationship between race and crime and between low income and crime," as Barbara Dafoe Whitehead noted in her famous "Dan Quayle was Right" article [*Atlantic Monthly*, 1993].

William Niskanen, chairman of the Cato Institute, observes that most variables that are said to determine the crime rate have not changed since 1960. Male unemployment, the poverty rate, and the percentage of church members has stayed approximately the same. Urbanization has increased slightly but hardly enough to explain crime surge. Since 1960, real personal income per capita doubled, and so has the number of police per capita. "The one condition that has changed substantially," Niskanen writes, "is the percentage of births [to] single mothers, increasing to 5 percent in 1960 [and] to 28 percent in 1991." (And . . . to an even higher rate in 1999.)

There is another association between illegitimacy and crime: unwed fathers are more likely to commit crimes than are married fathers. If you see two young men walking towards you on a lonely, dark street, you may start to worry. But if one of the men is holding the hand of a small child, your worries vanish. Marriage and mating really do civilize men, but mere sex and reproduction do not.

The Problem with Welfare

Although misguided welfare policies helped spur the rise in illegitimacy, the continued growth in illegitimacy, notwithstanding welfare reform in 1996, suggests a widespread breakdown in social mores, extending far beyond the ranks of welfare recipients. How to fix that problem is the most important question for persons who care about crime control in the long run. Compared to the disaster of illegitimacy, almost everything else on today's "anti-crime" agenda is a trivial distraction.

Speaking at the 1999 National Rifle Association (NRA) Convention in Denver, the late Vikki Buckley (Colorado's Secretary of State) brought the crowd to its feet when she explained: "Those who would run the NRA out of town need to look at our own children who are engaging in irresponsible sex and having children they cannot take care of. Such irresponsible sex is a new age hate crime—raise as much heck about that as you do the NRA and you will save more lives in 5 years than are taken with guns in a century."

Periodical Bibliography

The following articles have been selected to supplement the diverse views presented in this chapter. Addresses are provided for periodicals not indexed in the *Readers' Guide to Periodical Literature*, the *Alternative Press Index*, the *Social Sciences Index*, or the *Index to Legal Periodicals and Books*.

Sandra Arbetter
"Violence—A Growing Threat," *Current Health*, February 1995. Available from Weekly Reader Corporation, 200 First Stamford Place, PO Box 120023, Stamford, CT 06912.

Gregory J. Boyle
"More Punishment: Simple but Senseless," *Los Angeles Times*, February 24, 1997. Available from Times Mirror Square, Los Angeles, CA 90053.

Patrick Fagan
"The Real Root Cause of Violent Crime," *Vital Speeches of the Day*, December 15, 1995. Available from PO Box 1247, Mount Pleasant, SC 29465.

Richard Lacayo
"Toward the Root of Evil," *Time*, April 6, 1998.

Paul Lachine
"The Long Road After Littleton," *Christianity Today*, June 14, 1999.

Toni Locy
"Like Mother, Like Daughter," *U.S. News & World Report*, October 4, 1999.

Iain Murray
"Juvenile Murders: Guns the Least of It," *Christian Science Monitor*, March 27, 2000.

David W. Neuendorf
"What Is Behind the School Killings?" *Aurora Journal-Press*, 1998. Available from Register Publications, 126 West High St., Lawrenceberg, IN 47025.

Katha Pollitt
"Natural Born Killers," *Nation*, August 2, 1999.

Faraz Rana
"Violently Objecting to Media Critics," *University Wire*, October 6, 2000. Available from *Cavalier Daily*, University of Virginia, PO Box 400703, Charlottesville, VA 22904-4703.

Bruce Shapiro
"The Guns of Littleton," *Nation*, May 17, 1999.

Ken C. Winters
"Kids and Drugs: Treatment Recognizes Link Between Delinquency and Substance Abuse," *Corrections Today*, October 1998.

CHAPTER 3

What Factors Contribute to Gang-Related Juvenile Crime?

Chapter Preface

Since the explosion of crack cocaine sales in the 1980s, street gangs have increased in membership and location. What was once seen as an inner-city menace has now spread to rural neighborhoods and schools. Among the many theories regarding the causes of youth involvement in criminal street gangs is the argument that the media glorify the attitude and image of gang members. Many contend that the commercial marketing of trends and styles typically associated with gangsters influences juveniles to imitate their criminal behavior. According to Suren Pillay, an expert in political studies, "The attitude of African-American youth resonates because it speaks a discourse of alienation, but is given cultural power by the media." By selling the "bad boy" image of gangsters, many argue that society may be exacerbating the problem of criminal street gangs.

Others contend that juveniles who lack a solid and supportive family structure seek the camaraderie and loyalty found in a gang. According to John King, a police captain in Maryland, "Gangs provide a sense of belonging and fraternity." Many gang members come from single-parent families, abusive families, or have been involved in the foster care system for much of their lives. These children find a supportive family within the often destructive gang lifestyle.

Other factors that may influence gang-related juvenile crime include the violent lyrics of gangsta rap music, poverty, and the competition inherent in American capitalism. These are among the theories discussed in the following chapter.

"African-American alienation has become a highly marketable 'attitude' that permeates the sports industry as well as the music industry."

The Media Contribute to Gang-Related Juvenile Crime

Suren Pillay

In the following viewpoint, Suren Pillay argues that the film, music, and sports industries contribute to the problem of juvenile gang violence by portraying antisocial values in a positive light. In addition, because these industries advertise their clothes, music, and other products in ways that glamorize the gang lifestyle, they influence young, inexperienced teenagers into adopting a life of crime and violence. Pillay is a senior lecturer on political studies at the University of the Western Cape in South Africa.

As you read, consider the following questions:

1. According to the author, to what three factors do social scientists, community workers, and clergy attribute gangsterism?
2. What does the author claim is the difference between films shown in working-class and suburban areas?
3. What does gangsterism represent, as stated by Pillay?

Reprinted, with permission, from Suren Pillay, "Gangsters 'Just Do It' Like Their Idols," *Weekly Mail and Guardian*, July 18, 1997.

G angsterism has been at the centre of much debate and discussion of late. Gang leaders have become peace crusaders and peace crusaders are breaking the law.

Social scientists, community workers and clergy have argued convincingly that gangsterism is a historical response by working-class communities to unemployment, poverty and loss of self-esteem. Sociologists say gangs provide a sense of belonging and community amongst youth. The solution, they argue, would therefore lie in solving the socio-economic problems of our society. Give people jobs and they won't rob and steal, and they won't sell drugs.

This argument does not explain the numbers of youth from middle- and upper-class families who are committing crime or serving time. It does not explain the esteem and status gangs enjoy among young people growing up with very little material discomfort. Much of the problem appears to lie with the culture that has spread across the globe: selling and celebrating anti-social heroes.

Film Heroes

Most of the output of American cinema illustrates this. Actors like Jean-Claude van Damme, Sylvester Stallone and Arnold Schwarzenegger portray singularly violent and destructive characters. These "heroes" are highly individualistic and anti-social. In the pursuit of a notion of "justice", they destroy half a town without a wince.

Even in good-cop genre movies it is not unusual to have an entire fleet of cars destroyed in the pursuit of a lone criminal, or a spectacular shoot-out in a busy centre crowded with hysterical people. The audience is focused on hero and not the helpless mass, which engenders pity, because it reflects the powerlessness of the audiences' lives.

Cinemas in working-class areas consistently screen movies of a particular genre—dominated by [violent action]—while those in the plush suburbs are the "art-house" cinemas.

Violence sells. Any analysis of the media industry will tell you that. But it sells only where it has an audience. The debate has been raging about the effect screened violence has on actual violence. It would be in the interests of only the multi-million-dollar movie industry to say that there is no relationship between the two.

Is it just a coincidence that more murders take place where audiences are fed a diet of violent cinema, than in the suburbs?

© Walt Carr. Reprinted with permission.

It seems, however, too mechanical to argue that viewers are simply a passive audience, they are also an active audience. They appropriate and situate images, values and actions within their own environment. Martin Scorcese may be portraying the mob in a way that shows how ruthless and brutal their power is, to make them unattractive, but the values appropriated by his audience might be the opposite.

Sports Heroes

Anti-humanist individualism is not only celebrated on [film]. It pervades another mega-industry: sport: American sports in particular are major sources of income for a whole series of subsidiary industries, from shoe and clothing manufacturers, to network screening rights. Michael Jordan, Dennis

Rodman, Charles Barkley and others are taken off the court and draped over sneakers, soft-drink cans and cereal boxes. Young people, in particular, rush to purchase these goods because they associate them with their heroes.

They don't only buy the goods, they also buy the values. Just do it. Don't think about the fact that it takes a month's salary to buy them, just do it. Or that workers are being exploited in South East Asia to make them. Just do it. Buy them. Nike admitted in a *Sports Illustrated* article in 1993 that it actively pursues athletes with a "bad-boy attitude" to represent it. African-American alienation has become a highly marketable "attitude" that permeates the sports industry as well as the music industry. The profits reaped off gangsta rap is a useful illustration of this.

Gangster Heroes

The romanticised "hood" is now appropriated from the Bronx to Bonteheuwel, South Africa. Rap artists interpret their reality through historical constructs of alienated African-American youth. The "attitude" of African-American youth resonates because it speaks a discourse of alienation, but is given cultural power by the media and financial interests which have appropriated its symbols. This has been occurring over a period extending well into the early gang formations and their idealised gangster heroes.

Gangsterism is not a new problem, but it is not only an economically motivated phenomenon. It has taken on an internal sociological dynamic that spans generations, that represents an identity that articulates the values of radical individualism as opposed to collective and social responsibility.

Gangsterism represents the expression of the individualism of liberal society in its most alienated and stark form. The private power wielded behind the closed doors of city boardrooms might be more dangerous to us in the long run.

> *"This is the music du jour of many young North American teenagers these days—the evocation of sexual abuse, violence and death."*

Gangsta Rap Music Contributes to Gang-Related Juvenile Crime

Paul Palango

While many contend that rap music is a harmless form of entertainment and artistic expression, others argue that its violent content, degradation of women, and glorification of the gang lifestyle contribute to juvenile involvement in gangs and gang-related crime. In the following viewpoint, freelance journalist Paul Palango describes one teenage girl's descent into gang membership and prostitution. According to Palango, she maintains that the lyrics in rap music encouraged her involvement with gangs and contributed to her rebellion and delinquency.

As you read, consider the following questions:
1. What was the first clue to the changes in Kathleen?
2. How does the author define the term "disinhibited"?
3. According to Carey MacLellan, how do delinquent girls differ from delinquent boys?

Reprinted, with permission, from Paul Palango, "Danger Signs," *Maclean's*, December 18, 1997.

What first scares many parents is the music. Their daughter has just become a teenager and almost overnight, it seems, her taste has changed from Raffi to gangsta rap, the street music of the black ghettos in the United States. The little girl who once rollicked to Baby Beluga and Down by the Bay has, at the age of 12 or 13, become desperate to attract boys and win acceptance from other girls. She's taking endless showers to lyrics such as these from the popular *High School High* movie sound track: "Blow your head off"; "Let's get it on like Smith and Wesson"; "Kill a nigger for my nigger"—and far worse.

This is the music du jour of many young North American teenagers these days—the evocation of sexual abuse, violence and death. But the music usually is only a manifestation of something more sinister, lurking deep inside many young girls. For the damaged and insecure, the songs serve as a diabolical road map to the girls' own private hell.

Troubled Teenagers

Many come from dysfunctional families. Many are the daughters of alcohol and drug abusers, or have been physically or sexually abused, or, according to recent medical research, have suffered undetected brain injuries from childhood accidents.

Unable to function properly in society, these girls have low self-esteem, [and suffer] taunting and bullying [from classmates] at school. It is not a new phenomenon. It happens every year, in the meanest housing projects and the fanciest private schools. There is even a fascinating 1996 film about the subject, *Welcome to the Dollhouse*. The central character is a homely girl named Dawn Wiener who is so desperate for affection that she shows up repeatedly to meet a bad boy who keeps threatening to rape her—but, in the end, even he rejects her. . . .

Meet Kathleen. [She] came from a middle-class family in the Ottawa, Canada, area. Tall and gangly, and with a poor self-image, she had studied ballet as a child, but never excelled at anything. She had been sexually abused as a small child, although her family was unaware of it until after she hit bottom in a descent that began in Grade 9. She was 14, and found she couldn't successfully compete for the attention of boys. Older, bigger and tougher girls began to taunt and bully her. Kathleen stopped going to school and began hanging out in coffee shops and at the mall.

She took refuge in gangsta rap. Her favorites were Niggers With Attitude, Public Enemy and Ice T, whose narcotic-like chants and rhythms masked the malevolence of their lyrics. Their songs were paeans to violence, to killing police and degrading women.

Danger Signs

The clues to Kathleen's descent were subtle at first, lost in the confusion of hormonal change and the widely held myth that most teenagers instantly become rebellious once they turn 13. The first tip-off might have been when Kathleen shed her old and dear childhood friends. Although this change might not seem abnormal for someone moving from elementary to high school, experts say it is often the first visible marker in the destabilization of a personality. "I started to see them as Goody Two-shoes and nerds," Kathleen says. "On Friday nights, they stayed home and watched videos. I started hanging around with a girl who drank, but that was about it. She wasn't really a bad person." The friendship did not last long, however. Soon, Kathleen took up with Fay, a tougher, streetwise girl who not only drank but also did drugs. This tiered descent from childhood friends to unstable street acquaintances is typical of psychologically distressed teenagers, according to Richmond Hill, Ontario, behavioral specialist Ruth Whitham.

Unlike Kathleen, Fay came from a broken home. Her mother had been married four times and had run an escort service out of their house. Fay became Kathleen's mentor and guide to the underworld. As she looks back at herself now, Kathleen remembers having no emotions—an almost sociopathic view of the world. "I had no respect for or fear of authority," she recalls. And, she says, she was completely "disinhibited"—a clinical term to describe a person who is incapable of feeling embarrassment or shame. "I would do and say anything. I didn't give a damn."

Kathleen adopted the culture depicted in the rap songs as

her own. That culture grew out of grinding poverty, the lack of a political voice and the oppression of white police. Yet the rebellion and rage of the ghettos hold a curious appeal for some vulnerable nonblack teens. "We really got into this black thing," Kathleen says. "It's funny. I'm fair-skinned, but I desperately wanted to be black. I started dressing like a home-girl and talking the talk. When I was 14, I even told my mother that my goal was to have a baby with a black guy by the time I was 15."

Teaching Hatred

Although crime and hate have been an ongoing side effect of the rock music, the Rap sound has mushroomed crime in the areas of the gang concept. Even small towns are now being affected, and Rap stars have become the teachers of these gangs. This type of music is one of the largest reasons for the recent upsurge of racial tension and fear in the streets. Such social fires are being fed by these rhythmic proclaimers of hatred and violence.

Hubert T. Spence, *Confronting Contemporary Christian Music.* Dunn, NC: Foundations Press, 1997.

As the pattern of collapse continued, the shoplifting began. "It wasn't because I couldn't afford the clothes, because I could," she says. "I stole clothes to wear to the clubs—short skirts and bra tops that my mother wouldn't let me wear." Kathleen and Fay also hooked up with a group of criminally minded men, most of them black. She would go back to their apartments, do drugs, have sex and allow herself to be flattered. Desperately in need of love and acceptance, she was an all-too-willing victim.

The Ottawa street scene in the early to mid-1990s was typical of what was happening in other Canadian and U.S. cities. Out of nowhere violent gangs, many of them female, arose, with names such as the Scorpions, Nasty Girls and Bitches With Attitude. Kathleen became intimate with the gang world. "All you do is think about yourself, but you have no real feelings or emotions," she says. "No conscience and no judgment. I desperately wanted to be popular and the way to be popular was to do anything the gang leader wanted. If a guy told me I was pretty, I would go to bed with him. If my gang leader told me to beat someone up, I beat them up. I was always trying to feel tough and superior. After a while, you start to believe that you actually are the people in the songs."

Back to Reality

Kathleen hit bottom when she was 15. Her gang leader had ordered her to become a prostitute on the streets of Ottawa. "I only did it two times before my parents realized what was going on and took control." After a brief stay in an Ottawa detention centre, she was sent to a rehabilitation centre in Minnesota that specializes in psychiatry and addiction. "My mom told me it was going to be like a Holiday Inn, but it was like a jail," Kathleen says. "They brainwashed me—but it was for the good. They made me feel guilty. I got my judgment and conscience back.". . .

Having put those days behind her, [she has] changed her life around almost as completely as her hairstyle and clothes. That is not untypical, says Kathleen's lawyer, Carey MacLellan, who over the years has represented many youths in criminal matters. "For girls, there is an intensity to their involvement, a completeness that is different from boys. More often than not, a boy will be involved in crime but will also be hanging around school and doing a little schoolwork with some degree of normalcy. When it comes to changing their behavior, boys talk about changing, but it's usually only a lot of lip service," MacLellan notes. "The girls tend to go right at it. When they make up their mind to change, they change completely.". . .

Today, Kathleen is in university, doing exceptionally well, and hopes one day to become a police officer. "I look back at those days and the influence the rap music had on me, and I can't believe how I could have been influenced," she says. "It was all about the degradation of women, but I couldn't see that at the time."

Kathleen's middle-class parents had the money and connections to save her. But, says MacLellan, "for every one who does change, there are a hundred who aren't functioning very well in society."

"A lot of kids think that the only way they will ever have a real family is to join a gang."

A Need for Family Contributes to Gang-Related Juvenile Crime

Anonymous

Experts claim that one of the many motivating factors for youth gang involvement is the unfulfilled need for a sense of family. Many juvenile gang members are products of broken homes or victims of child abuse who end up in the foster care system. In the following viewpoint, the anonymous author speaks with three teenagers involved with gangs, each of whom expresses a familial sense of belonging to the gang and with the other gang members. This viewpoint was excerpted from *Foster Care Youth United*, a bimonthly newsletter written by and for young people in the foster care system and produced by the organization Youth Communication.

As you read, consider the following questions:
1. What reason does Taz give for wanting to join a gang?
2. What are the three things Joseph claims to have gained by joining the Latin Kings?
3. What does the author consider to be a solution for the problem of gangs?

Excerpted from Anonymous, "The Real Deal on Gangs," *Youth Communication*, November 12, 1998. Reprinted with permission from New Youth Connections; copyright 1998 by Youth Communication, 224 W. 29th St., 2nd Floor, New York, NY 10001.

B loods, Latin Kings, Crips. It seems as if we can't go at least one day without the topic of gang violence or murder entering our heads. And with all of the bad things that we have heard about gangs (like how they slice you for wearing their gang colors, or kill people for no reason), I couldn't imagine anyone wanting to join a gang.

But although gangs are feared, there is little that is known about them. It was very difficult for me to find gang members who were willing to talk.

But when I finally found those teenagers, they had a lot to say. And some of what they had to say might change your views on gangs.

More and more young people may be joining gangs, but nobody really knows why these children are joining. I asked Joseph, 18, who lives in a group home and is a Latin King. "[Me and my family] were having a lot of fights. I really wasn't getting any love from them."

Family Problems

I talked to Gerard (whose "organization" name is "Crazy Blood"), a 16-year-old who also lives in a group home, and is a member of the Bloods. When asked what was going on in his family life that made him want to join a gang, he said, "My mom's was flipping. She was telling me to do things that I didn't want to do. So I was like f-ck it. I was getting money [from my mom's] but I just started hustling with my dogs."

And I had the pleasure of talking to a 16-year-old female who prefers to be called "Taz." Taz is not a gang member, but wants to join. When I asked her why, she said, "The Bloods are all about being a family, sticking together, going out for theirs and getting that dough. And that is what I'm all about."

But not all teenagers join gangs because of family problems. Napz, a 17-year-old male who is down with the gang known as La Familia, when asked if he joined his organization because of family problems, simply said, "My family life and my life was good."

If your family life is good, there are other reasons why people join gangs. Joseph said, "[The Latin Kings] are always there for me when I have beef."

By this short but straight-to-the-point quote, I got the

understanding that many teenagers join because they need someone to help them out when they get into physical confrontations. Taz finalized my conclusion: "You will always have someone to look out for you, and to be there for you when you need them."

Peer Pressure

As the number of teen gang members becomes larger and larger, I wonder: Is it is really that easy to get into a gang? I mean, if you want to join, do you just say, "Can I be in your gang?"

When I asked the "experts," they shed some light on the subject.

"I grew up with Latin Kings," said Joseph. "They asked

Home Away from Home

Many [teenagers] see gang membership as a way of acquiring power and protection from the crime and violence they fear in their communities. But the primary draw of gangster "families" is their offer of the identity, acceptance, security, and attention so many kids are not getting at home. Black street gangs will call each other "cuz" for "cousin." And gang members' loyalty to one another, even unto death, presents a strong appeal to abused or neglected children.

A 1995 Heritage Foundation survey showed that a substantial majority of teenaged criminals are from broken and single-parent households. In gangs, the older male leader often functions as a surrogate father—from whom his devoted "homeboys" will accept parent-like discipline and even punishment. "Gangs provide a sense of belonging and fraternity," says John King, a Maryland police captain. The paradox, he added, "is that the gang's approach for achieving these things is illegal and destructive to the gang member, the family unit and the community."

Former president Lyndon Johnson said: "The family is the cornerstone of society. . . . When the family collapses, it is the children who are usually damaged. When it happens on a massive scale, the community itself is crippled." Today we are seeing the result of our crippled society in the massive rise of gangs that—tragically—give children a home away from the home their parents have failed to build.

Rosaline Bush and Nina George Hacker, *Family Voice*, February, 1997.

---

me if I wanted to be down with the nation."

"People kept on asking me to join. Family members, cousins and my best friends," said Napz.

"I used to hang out with a lot of [dogs], so they asked me to be down," said Gerard.

From these quotes, it seems like one of the reasons why teenagers join organizations is because they want to belong to something. When a teenager is asked to be in a gang, it is like being asked to join a private party. It makes you feel like you're special.

"We're Like a Family"

Sometimes the love that teenagers get from gangs is greater than the love that they receive from their own families.

"We're like a family. We do sh-t together, we get money together. I'm going to bang for my dogs and they are going to bang for me," said Gerard.

But I wasn't satisfied with just one opinion. So I went to Joseph and asked him if he considered the Latin Kings to be like a family. He said, "Well, they are not like my family, they are my family."

Taz said if she joined the Bloods, she would "get the satisfaction of having another family."

With these three quotes, I put three and three together. Joseph, Gerard and Taz are all in the foster care system and they are all in gangs. Are these teens trying to recover a missing part of family that was lost a long time ago? Are they creating their own family because they honestly don't have a family? I came to the conclusion that a lot of kids think that the only way they will ever have a real family is to join a gang.

Joseph told me that by joining the Latin Kings he gained acceptance, love and respect. These are things that most teenagers should be receiving at home. But instead, some have to sink as low as joining a gang. . . .

Solutions?

For a problem as big as gangs, there really isn't any solution, but there is always "prevention." If you are a parent and you don't give your child love at home, don't be surprised if you discover that your child is in a gang.

One of my final conclusions is that gang life is not as easy as everyone I interviewed made it seem. It is true that you do get another family. And from my experience hanging out with gangs, I can add that kids in a gang are regular people.

But the lives they lead are far from any life that should be led.

"Children who are physically, sexually, or emotionally abused or abandoned by their parents develop low self-esteem and are more prone to commit acts of violence."

Poor Parenting Contributes to Gang-Related Juvenile Crime

Lewis Yablonsky

Many gang members cite an abusive home life as a contributing factor to their gang lifestyle and claim that violence in the home taught them to lash out at others in their environment. In the following viewpoint, sociologist Lewis Yablonsky concurs that poor parenting can lead children to gang activity. Yablonsky contends that violent, drug-abusing parents foster low self-esteem, a distrustful view of society, and such self-destructive behavior as joining a gang. Yablonsky is the author of *Gangsters: Fifty Years of Madness, Drugs, and Death on the Streets of America*, from which this viewpoint is excerpted.

As you read, consider the following questions:
1. According to the author, what basic ingredient to socialization is missing in youths who become sociopathic gangsters?
2. As cited by Yablonsky, how does Marshall Cherkas claim an infant will react to not having its needs adequately met?
3. Which type of discipline are substance-abusing parents most likely to administer, according to the author?

It is of value to analyze the causal factors that produce the sociopathic gangster. The following analysis reveals some of the family and parental socialization factors that help to create the gangster's sociopathic personality.

Family Impacts

An adequate social self develops from a consistent pattern of interaction with rational adult parents in a normative family socialization process. Effective adult role models, especially two parents, help a youth learn social feelings of love, compassion, and sympathy. This concept of adequate self-emergence through constructive social interaction with others, especially parents, is grounded in the theoretical and research findings of a number of social psychologists.

For example, sociologist G.H. Mead, on the issue of the proper personality development that results from effective parental socialization of a child, asserts,

> The self arises in conduct when the individual becomes a social object in experience to himself. This takes place when the individual assumes the attitude or uses the gestures which another individual (usually his parents) would use. Through socialization, the child gradually becomes a social being. The self thus has its origin in communication and in taking the role of the other.

Social psychologist Harry Stack Sullivan perceived the self as being made up of what he calls "reflected appraisals." According to Sullivan,

> The child lacks equipment and experience necessary for a careful and unclouded evaluation of himself. The only guides he has are those of the significant adults or others who take care of him and treat him with compassion. The child thus experiences and appraises himself in accordance with the reactions of parents and others close to him. By facial expressions, gestures, words, and deeds, they convey to him the attitudes they hold toward him, their regard for him or lack of it.

In brief, a set of positive sympathetic responses by socializing agents, usually the child's parents, are necessary for adequate self-growth. This component is generally absent in the development of youths who become sociopathic gangsters.

The basic ingredient, missing in most sociopathic gangsters' socialization, is a loving parent or adult. Based on extensive research, psychologists Joan and William McCord assert,

> Because the rejected child does not love his parents and they
> do not love him, no identification takes place. Nor does the
> rejected child feel the loss of love—a love which he never
> had—when he violates moral restriction. Without love from
> an adult socializing agent, the psychopath remains asocial.

Delinquents Versus Nondelinquents

Psychologists Edwin Megargee and Roy Golden carried out
extensive research cross-comparing psychopathic delinquent
youths, including gangsters, with a control group of nondelinquent youths. Based on their research they concluded
that sociopathic delinquents had a significantly poorer rela-
tion with their parents than nondelinquents; and the sociopathic delinquents had significantly more negative attitudes
toward their mothers and their fathers than those of nondelinquents.

Dr. Marshall Cherkas, an eminent psychiatrist, in his
thirty years of experience as a court psychiatrist interviewed
several hundred delinquent sociopaths, including a number
of gangsters. His conclusions about the origin of the sociopathic delinquent's personality summarizes the observations
of other theorists on the subject. I concur with the following
statement he presented to me in an interview on the causal
context of the sociopath's early family life experience:

> Children are extremely dependent upon nurturing parents
> for life's sustenance as well as satisfaction and avoidance of
> pain. In the earliest phase of life, in their first year, infants
> maintain a highly narcissistic position in the world. Their
> sense of security, comfort, reality, and orientation is focused
> on their own primitive needs with little awareness and real-
> ity testing of the external world. As the normal infant devel-
> ops, its security and comfort is reasonably assured. There oc-
> curs a natural attachment, awareness, and interest in "the
> Other." As the child matures, the dependency upon "the
> Other," its parents, diminishes, but the strength of the self is
> enhanced, and the child develops an awareness that its nar-
> cissistic needs are met through a cooperative, adaptive, and
> mutually supportive relationship to its parents and others. In
> other words, the child recognizes that even though its selfish
> (narcissistic) needs are extremely important, they can best be
> served by appropriately relating to other people, especially
> its parents.

Infants whose needs are not adequately met because of the parents' own exaggerated narcissistic needs develop feelings of mistrust, insecurity, and wariness about the capacities of their provider. In order to protect itself, the child may perform many tasks to gain attention, support, and interest from the parent. The child also begins to feel that it cannot trust others, and that its needs can only be met through self-interest. The child who cannot count on its own parents begins to become egocentric and therefore sociopathic in its behavior.

It Starts with Abuse

Based on my experience, I have determined that the basic reason for the sociopathic gangster's lack of trust noted by Cherkas and others is primarily a result of the physical, emotional, and sexual abuse that he has received from his parents in the context of his socialization process. The emotional abuse is often in the form of the absence of any socialization of the needs of the child or of outright abandonment.

The parental factor in the socialization of a gangster has several roots and implications. Children who are physically, sexually, or emotionally abused or abandoned by their parents develop low self-esteem and are more prone to commit acts of violence. They also denigrate themselves, feel worthless, and are less likely to care about what happens to them. These negative social-psychological forces contribute to the acting out of self-destructive behavior, including drug abuse and violent gangster behavior.

The Substance-Abusing Parent

Most youths who become sociopathic gangsters have parents who are alcoholics or drug addicts. In extreme cases, at birth they are physiologically affected by being born to a mother who is an addicted crack-cocaine, heroin, or alcohol user. These children are sometimes born addicted and have severe physiological and psychological deficits.

As most research and my own observations over the years have revealed, substance abuse is an egocentric problem. The drug addict or alcoholic is consumed with the machinations of his or her habit. In a significant sense, whether or not the parents have a sociopathic personality, their behavior in the throes of their addiction is self-centered and consequently sociopathic in their relationship to their child. This form of parenting is not conducive to effectively socializing a child into a caring, compassionate, loving person. Children who are socialized in the chaotic world of a substance-abusing family tend to have a limited trust of others, become egocentric, and acompassionate. These sociopathic personality factors facilitate their participation in the violent gang. In brief, based on this varied research and its theoretical implications, it can be concluded that the proper and functional adult role models necessary for adequate socialization are usually absent from the social environment of youths who become gangsters.

Most gangsters come from dysfunctional families with brutal or absentee fathers. The negative adult role model that a youth growing up without a father may emulate is often the "ghetto hustler"—a fixture in the black hood. Malcolm X in his autobiography described this type of negative role model as follows:

> The most dangerous black man in America is the ghetto hustler. . . . The ghetto hustler is internally restrained by nothing. He has no religion, no concept of morality, no civic responsibility, no fear—nothing. This type of individual's hustle may be drugs, and he is often a father who has abandoned his son.

Lack of Discipline

A significant factor in this cauldron of substance-abusing, negative parental impacts is related to ineffectual discipline. Essentially there are four basic forms of discipline in the socialization process of a child: strict, sporadic, lax, and none. Research reveals that the most damaging form is sporadic discipline. In this form the child seldom knows when he or she is right or wrong. Substance-abusing parents tend to administer this type of discipline. They are out of any parental loop most of the time; however, they randomly will appear with some form of discipline that is often not connected to their child's "bad behavior." Children subjected to this type of discipline tend to develop a dim view of justice in their life and the justice that exists in the larger society. The results of this pattern of sporadic discipline feeds into the sociopathic viewpoint of distrust of others and a gangster lifestyle.

The children of substance abusers are also influenced by their parents' lifestyle to accept drug use as a way of resolving their emotional pain. Following in the path of their parents' substance abuse becomes for the gangster a way of ameliorating their painful feelings of low self-esteem and their sense of hopelessness in life.

Family Factors

Family problems and parenting difficulties can increase the risk of kids joining gangs. Many kids who join gangs come from middle-class families with two biological parents at home. However, many of these youth come from homes that are deeply troubled. They seek from the gang what they are not getting (or will not accept) from their families. They are looking for acceptance, love, companionship, leadership, encouragement, recognition, respect, role models, rules, security, self-esteem, structure and a sense of belonging. When children's emotional needs are met in families, the results are positive; otherwise they may look to gangs, and the outcome is usually negative.

Herbert G. Lindgren, "Gangs: The New Family," *Family Life*, June 1996.

In my work with delinquents, especially in psychiatric facilities, I have observed the impact created by drug-abusing parents on hundreds of youths who develop sociopathic personalities and become gangsters.

One typical example is a thirteen-year-old [gang member] whose gang name was L.K., short for "Little Killer." L.K. was emotionally and physically abused from the age of four, several times a week, by his drug addict father. The physical beatings and verbal abuse administered by his father often had little relationship to L.K.'s good or bad behavior. He would be beaten or verbally abused for a variety of "offenses" chosen at random by his irrational father. His father assaulted whenever he had a need to act out his drug-induced personal frustrations with the world around him; a convenient target was his son and his wife. According to L.K.,

He would beat the shit out of me for no reason—just because he was loaded and mad at the world. I've always felt like a punching bag, or maybe more like a piece of shit. If my own father thinks I'm a punk and a loser, maybe that's what I am.

The Effects of Abuse

The irrational behavior of L.K.'s father led to several consequences. The indiscriminate physical and verbal abuse had the effect of producing low self-esteem in the youth. He tended to feel humiliated and worthless. As a result of these feelings, he thought he was a loser. The only place where he found he had power, respect, and a reasonable sense of self was with his homies in the Venice gang identified as the Insane Baby Crips. The gang gave L.K. some level of the positive approval he so desperately needed and sought.

L.K.'s typical dysfunctional family helped to create a sociopathic gangster in several ways. First, the youth had no one in his family he felt he could trust. Second, there were no significant people in L.K.'s basic socialization who were positive role models, demonstrating how a person shows love and compassion to another person. A child can't learn to be compassionate if he never sees any examples of caring in his crucial early years. Third, because he was abused by his father, L.K. developed a low self-concept. In a reaction to these feelings of inadequacy, he developed a macho-syndrome that he acted out in the gang as a "little killer." Fourth, the gang gave this emotionally needy youth some sense of self-respect and power in his chaotic world. All of these socialization factors converged to produce a violent sociopathic gangster.

"[Gangs] are acting out the behavior of a competitive and violent society that does not give priority to human needs."

American Capitalism Contributes to Gang-Related Juvenile Crime

Christian Smith

In an effort to deter gang-related crime, in 1997 Los Angeles courts approved injunctions against members of one of its most violent gangs, the 18th Street gang. As described in the following viewpoint, many of the gang members' most basic civil rights, such as the right to congregate on the street, were revoked as officials attempted to better control their actions. Christian Smith, a self-described radical therapist in North Hollywood, argues that not only are the injunctions unconstitutional, but they also ignore the fundamental factors that attract children to the gang lifestyle: poverty and competition. He maintains that American capitalism prioritizes profit over human life, and that gangs are a logical extension of this value system.

As you read, consider the following questions:
1. What, according to the author, is the "identified patient" of a family, and how does he relate this concept to the 18th Street gang?
2. How does the author compare business owners and landlords to gang members?
3. What are the four causes of gang violence, according to the author?

Reprinted, with permission, from Christian Smith, "Isolating Gang Members: A Prescription for More Violence," *Change-Links News*, October 1997, at www. labridge.com/change-links.

Judges, city attorneys, police and other members of our society charged with protecting [its citizens] us are seeking court injunctions to restrict the movements of the [Los Angeles based] 18th Street gang. The suspected gang members are not allowed to be in groups in the street. They are not allowed to talk on cellular phones, nor to move freely through their neighborhoods. It is hoped that by controlling their movements, the police will control the activity of the gang, which includes violent behavior. There is a fundamental contradiction in this approach that will ultimately create more violence. We are trying to control gang behavior as if it exists in a vacuum. Yet gangs play a role in the functioning of our society.

A revolution occurred in my field, psychotherapy, in the last decade. We came to understand that all behavior, including violence, occurs in the context of a family system. The person who ends up in therapy is simply the identified patient (IP) of his family. His/her role is to bind the anxiety and immature functioning of the entire family. This way the other members can point their fingers at the sick one and escape assuming the responsibility for creating a family with problems.

In the same fashion, the members of the 18th Street gang are the identified patients of our society. They are acting out the behavior of a competitive and violent society that does not give priority to human needs. If we stop pointing the finger at them and look at ourselves for a second, we would understand their violent behavior in its societal context.

Violent Entrepreneurs

As adults we have created a society in which 22% of our children live under the poverty line and 40% of Latino and 45.9% of Black children live in poverty. Under these conditions, doesn't it make sense for the youth to organize into extralegal business ventures-gangs? Legal businesses steal value from workers every day. They control territories just like gang members. The 18th Street gang is accused of using violence to control street corners and renting them out to drug peddlers. Can I also accuse landlords of controlling the land and renting it out to commodity peddlers? Can I get an injunction against the capitalist owners of my ancestors' land—Aztlan—for violent expropriation of territory? Why are white collar capitalist gangs allowed to plunder the world (using their cellular phones to call in the acquisitions to their stock brokers), while tattooed cholo entrepreneurs have their constitutional rights taken away?

© Matt Matteo. Reprinted with permission.

"It's because they're violent," you say. Gangs kill innocent children who stray in the way of their turf wars. O.K., I agree that blowing people away sucks. Now what about our government that has shown our kids that when we disagree with someone we have the option to blow them up. Why is a drive-by shooting any different than the invasion of Panama? Our government is one of the most violent in the world, spending 326.1 billion dollars a year on weapons—27% of the world's military expenditures. Our government has blown away millions of innocent people throughout its bloody history. It makes sense that some people will learn from the government to organize themselves into warring groups competing for territory in a city in the same fashion as the U.S. government violently competes for territory in the world.

Gangs as a Creation of Society

Gangs are a logical development in our society. They are the product of violence, competition and alienation. They are also brotherhoods for many kids who have been thrown out of society. Gangs take better care of their members than the government takes care of its citizens.

Isolating the 18th Street gang and stripping them of their constitutional rights will only create more alienation and violence amongst these fellow citizens of our city. They are not monsters. They are humans like you and I. In fact they are like they are because of the society that you and I created. It's time to stop pointing our fingers at the gangs and ask ourselves how we contribute to the chaos and violence in our society. We must explore the role of poverty, competition and the prioritization of profit over human needs in the creation of gangs.

The function of the efforts that we put into controlling gangs is to distract us from the real causes of gang violence—poverty, alienation, deteriorating social relationships and societal violence. It is instructive to stand back and see the entire picture. Capitalists and their puppets in government along with an obedient population, create the inhuman conditions of capitalism. The resultant poverty and social violence rips through our communities laying waste to generations of people. Some of these people organize themselves into extralegal groupings—gangs. They protect themselves and their investments with violence. Then the original persecutors—capitalists—attack the victims of their system of artificial scarcity with police and court injunctions. Blaming the gangs allows capitalist oppression to remain unnoticed. If we unite behind the government to stop the "hoodlums" we won't notice the government's truncheon as it crashes down on our social programs and our human rights.

We need to listen to the message that gangs are sending us and use it to explore our society. We must treat the entire family if we are to be successful in stopping the violence. If we do not do this, we will allow the society that creates gangs and violence to continue it's production uninterrupted. The court injunction [approved in 1997] against the 18th Street gang is a prescription for more violence.

Periodical Bibliography

The following articles have been selected to supplement the diverse views presented in this chapter. Addresses are provided for periodicals not indexed in the *Readers' Guide to Periodical Literature*, the *Alternative Press Index*, the *Social Sciences Index*, or the *Index to Legal Periodicals and Books*.

Kathy Braidhill	"Where the Boyz Are," *Los Angeles Magazine*, January 1998.
Rosaline Bush and Nina George Hacker	"Kids Without a Conscience," *Family Voice*, February 1997. Available from Concerned Women for America, 1015 15th St. NW, Suite 1100, Washington, DC 20005.
Mike Clements	"Adult Absence Can Lead Kids to Join Gangs," *Panama City News Herald*, March 19, 2000. Available from PO Box 68, Panama City, FL 32402.
Gary Delgado	"Warriors for Peace: Stopping Youth Violence with Barrios Unidos," *Colorlines*, Winter 1999.
Leigh Dyer and Eric Frazier	"Gangs' Allure Growing," *Charlotte Observer*, October 16, 1999. Available from 600 Tryon, Charlotte, NC, 28202.
Jan Golab	"The Color of Hate," *Los Angeles Magazine*, November 28, 1999.
Richard Grant	"Dial Eme for Murder," *Los Angeles Magazine*, May 1997.
Karina Ioffee	"Why Youth Gangs Are Snaring Children of Recent Immigrants," *Eastbay Express*, November 26, 1999. Available from PO Box 3198, Berkeley, CA 94703-0198.
Dan Macallair	"The Drop in Gang-Related Killing," *Orange County Register*, January 9, 2000. Available from PO Box 11944, Santa Ana, CA 92711.
Sarah McNaught	"Gangsta Girls," *Boston Phoenix*, May 20, 1999. Available from 126 Brookline Ave., Boston, MA 02215.
Armando Morales	"The Homicide-Suicide Link of Adolescent Gang Culture," *Denver Post*, May 16. 1999. Available from 1560 Broadway, Denver, CO 80202.
Michelle Shephard	"Teen Gangs: Fear in Our Schools," *Toronto Star*, October 24, 1998. Available from 1 Yonge St., Toronto, Ontario MSE 1E6 Canada.

Damon A. Vangelis   "Self-Destructive Tendencies: The 'Gangsta Rap' Industry," *Williams Free Press*, 1996. Available from the Zenger Foundation, PO Box 401, Williamstown, MA 01267.

Gordon Witkin   "Swift and Certain Punishment," *U.S. News & World Report*, December 29, 1997.

CHAPTER 4

How Can Juvenile Crime and Violence Be Combated?

Chapter Preface

Recently, authorities have tried various means of addressing the problem of juvenile crime including teenage curfew laws, parental responsibility laws, and after-school and early intervention programs. The outrage over serious, violent offenses committed by juveniles has revived criminal procedures deemed unjust in 1899, when the Illinois Juvenile Court Act established the nation's first juvenile justice system. Its purpose was to eliminate the brutality inflicted upon children within the adult justice system and to provide facilities dedicated to rehabilitation, instead of incarceration. Recently, however, many argue that juvenile offenders who commit adult crimes ought to withstand the adult punishment.

Many supporters of adult punishments for juveniles argue that the juvenile justice system enables children to commit crimes by exacting minor punishments as well as expunging juveniles' records when they turn eighteen. As a *Newsday* editorial states, "Right now the system is riddled with loopholes that allow too many kids to skate. That's no good for the public, no good for the victims, many of whom are themselves kids, and no good for delinquents who, unchecked, can drift into ever-more-destructive behavior."

On the other hand, proponents of the juvenile justice system believe that harsher punishments of juveniles turn potentially productive members of society into vicious criminals. One argument against trying juveniles as adults is that teens are likely to commit more crimes after serving adult sentences. According to Jason Ziedenberg and Vincent Schiraldi, "A substantial body of research shows that placing youths in adult institutions accentuates criminal behavior after release." Not only do many delinquents end up back in detention or prison after release, but they also end up brutalized by the guards or other inmates while serving that time. Advocates of the juvenile justice system argue that keeping children away from adult felons is a more effective way to ensure they develop into productive citizens.

Whether children should be incarcerated with adults is one of the issues discussed in this chapter on how to combat juvenile crime.

"It's time to take juvenile crime more seriously and start treating these criminals in the more just adult court."

More Juveniles Should Be Tried as Adults

Hanna Chiou

As a response to the increased lethality of juvenile crime, many states are implementing legislation allowing underage criminals to be tried and punished as adults. These policies result in harsher sentences and possible incarceration with adults in state prisons, sparking controversy over the ethics of punishing juveniles so severely. Advocates of such punishments claim that teenagers know the difference between right and wrong and have the maturity to make competent decisions. Hanna Chiou makes this argument in the following viewpoint. She contends that the damage caused by a young criminal is equal to that caused by an adult and should result in the same punishment. Chiou works at Lynbrook High School in California and is a staff writer for DigitalHigh.com, an online forum created by and for teenagers in the Silicon Valley.

As you read, consider the following questions:
1. According to Chiou, in what age group has crime increased 160 percent from 1984 to 1999?
2. What does Chiou suggest may be a mitigating circumstance in determining criminal responsibility?
3. What problem does Chiou have with the current standard of determining maturity by age?

Reprinted, with permission, from "Adult Crimes Deserve Adult Treatment," by Hanna Chiou, *Digital High*, 2000.

Thursday, May 21, 1998. In Springfield, Oregon, 15-year old Kip Kinkel opened fire in the cafeteria of Thurston High School. Two were killed and 25 others were wounded.

Tuesday, March 24, 1998. In Jonesboro, Arkansas, 11-year old Andrew Golden and 13-year old Mitchell Johnson pulled the fire alarm and shot at the students filing out of the school. Five were killed and ten were wounded.

Monday, Dec. 1, 1997. In Paducah, Kentucky, 14-year old Michael Carneal pulled out a pistol and began firing on a student prayer group. Three were killed and five others were wounded.

These incidents are only a tiny sample of the school shootings that have been committed by juveniles in the United States. More shootings have happenned in Onalaska, Washington; Johnston, Rhode Island; Endinboro, Pennsylvania; St. Charles, Missouri . . . the list goes on and on!

The criminals of today just seem to be getting younger and younger. According to the Iowa State Daily [a daily newspaper issued by Iowa State University], "Murder cases among 14- to 17-year olds have increased 160 percent between 1984 and 1999." Unfortunately, these 14- to 17-year olds are still classified as juveniles, and thus, are tried in the juvenile court, a legislative system that prosecutes these criminals more leniently due to their age "immaturity." Looking at these statistics, I say that it's time to take juvenile crime more seriously and start treating these criminals in the more just adult court.

Mental Maturity or Immaturity Cannot Be Gauged by Age

Lynbrook [High School] junior Stephanie Tsai disagrees with this saying, "At the age of 18, teens are allowed to vote because people believe that by that age they can think rationally and sensibly. Until kids are 18, they cannot be held responsible for their actions." Let's examine this age 18 issue more closely. . . .

Granted, our society does give juveniles the right to vote at age 18. However, many states give them the right to drive at age 16 and the right to drink at age 21. The fact is that declaring an 18-year-old an adult is an arbitrary standard to determine maturity as far as prosecuting crime goes.

The juvenile court system was originally implemented to protect juveniles from the "harsh" adult court, for juvenile criminals were thought to be more mentally "immature" than adults. This may very well be if we were speaking of a 6-year-old. However, 17-year-olds classify as juveniles as well. Are we to say that 17-year-olds are significantly more "immature" and should "not be held responsible for their actions" than that of an adult 18-year old?

Adult Time for Adult Crime

We ought to hold young criminals more responsible for their behavior, punishing violent juveniles like adults. Parents ought to take more responsibility for their children. And communities ought to take more responsibility for steering their young people away from crime and drugs. . . .

[We also need to] toughen punishment for violent juveniles. We can no longer tolerate violent criminal behavior by juveniles. We have got to get tough with these young thugs. . . .

[We must also] punish adult crimes with adult time. We should mandate that 14- and 15-year olds who commit violent crimes be tried as adults.

James B. Hunt, "Agenda for Action: Crime Fighting Plan," February 3, 1998.

Furthermore, if our justice system uses mental incompetency as the reason juveniles have their own separate and more lenient court, why aren't 40-year-olds with the mind of a 10-year-old prosecuted in the juvenile justice system? Are they not mentally "immature" as well?

Adult Courts Ensure Basic Freedoms for Juveniles

An incorrect assumption about this controversial matter is if the juvenile were to be prosecuted in the adult court, he would be condemned with an adult sentence. Wrong. Referring back to the 40-year-old criminal with a 10-year-old mind. The reason he would be prosecuted in the adult system despite his mental immaturity is because these courts do allow for mitigating circumstances such as mental incompetency. The same goes for juveniles. If a 15-year-old were truly mentally immature, the adult justice system would take that fact into account of its decision and ruling.

Furthermore, while others may argue that the juvenile justice system has the juvenile's best interests in mind, basic freedoms such as due process are denied in the juvenile courts. While those prosecuted in adult courts are entitled to a jury, juvenile sentences usually lay in the hands of an individual judge.

Juveniles Inflict as Much Damage as Adult Offenders

The simple fact is that fully competent and mature juveniles are fully capable of committing the same crime as a competent adult. The results of the crime are the same. In burglary, an innocent person was robbed of his possessions. In murder, an innocent person was robbed of his life. As Katrina Ng, Santa Clara University freshman answered, "If they commit the adult crimes, they should pay the adult consequences. It's not as if they don't know the difference between right and wrong."

And even in the extreme cases where right and wrong were indistinguishable to the immature juvenile, the adult justice system would be better equipped to prosecute him, allowing for mitigating circumstances and giving due process. This way, justice is best achieved—on both sides.

> *"You don't have to be an expert in criminal justice policy to understand that a teenager who is brutalized in prison will probably not metamorphose into a productive, law-abiding citizen."*

Juveniles Should Not Be Tried as Adults

Wendy Kaminer

In response to recent incidents of violent juvenile crime, legislators have considered trying and punishing dangerous minors as adults. Opponents to this practice allege that incarcerating children in prisons will not only result in their brutal abuse at the hands of adults, but also in an increased rate of arrests after release. In the following viewpoint, Wendy Kaminer makes this argument. She contends that assistance programs for high school diplomas or job training are more effective at reducing crime than harsher punishments. Kaminer is a lawyer, author, and senior correspondent for the *American Prospect*.

As you read, consider the following questions:
1. According to the author, what changes does the Juvenile Crime Control Act of 1997 implement in the juvenile justice system?
2. What does Kaminer consider to be the most dangerous aspect of the new legislation?
3. What kinds of incentives and disincentives does the Boston Gun Project offer, according to the author?

Reprinted, with permission, from Wendy Kaminer, "Sending Kids to Jail," *IntellectualCapital.com*, May 15, 1997.

V iolent juvenile crime is particularly chilling. We're not supposed to be afraid of our children. Fostered partly by the proliferation of guns, juvenile violence rose in the late 1980s through the early 1990s, shaping a sensational, popular image of teenage sociopaths running wild. Very occasional, but highly-publicized acts of violence by children under 13 engendered a belief that even grade school kids can be irredeemable. Today, although the juvenile crime rate remains high, it is in decline, largely because of a recent drop in violent crime by young offenders. Still, the fearful sense that we are besieged by youthful predators persists.

The Lock 'Em Up Approach

Exploiting these fears, the House of Representatives recently approved "The Juvenile Crime Control Act of 1997," which would greatly increase the number of children tried as adults and incarcerated in adult facilities. Pursuant to this bill, adult prosecutions of 14-year-olds charged with violent felonies and drug offenses would be mandatory in federal court. Federal prosecutors would have the discretion to initiate adult prosecutions against 13-year-olds.

Most juvenile crime, however, is prosecuted in state court; changes in federal penal law are largely symbolic. The thrust of the House bill is its radical revising of state juvenile justice systems: In order to receive federal funds, states would have to follow federal rules mandating the adult treatment of juveniles 15 and older who are charged with serious, violent crimes and the repeal of confidentiality rules regarding juvenile proceedings. States also would be required to impose sanctions on children for every delinquent act and to allow prosecutions of parents or guardians of delinquents. (So much for devolution.)

The treatment of allegedly violent juveniles as adults is not new: States began adult prosecutions of kids charged with homicides and other serious felonies in the 1980s. In general, these experiments don't seem to have succeeded. Studies of Florida, New York and New Jersey show that recidivism rates are higher among juveniles prosecuted as adults than among those tried in juvenile court for similar crimes. And, most states have not chosen to adopt the extremely punitive treatment of juvenile offenders mandated by the House. Only an estimated 5 to 12 states would now qualify for federal funds under the House bill.

A Cruel Punishment

What is most dangerous about the new juvenile justice bill is the promised incarceration of juveniles with adult offenders. It would effectively sentence children to be raped. Minors in adult facilities are five times more likely to be sexually assaulted than are minors in juvenile facilities—as if the incidence of rape in juvenile facilities weren't horrible enough. An estimated 45,000 boys are sexually assaulted in prison every year, according to Stephen Donaldson of Stop Prisoner Rape. In adult prisons, Donaldson estimates that some 65,000 sexual victimizations occur daily, considering the number of men forced into prostitution by their "protectors." Nearly 300,000 incarcerated boys and men are raped in every year. The most vulnerable inmates are the youngest, weakest, least experienced.

A minority of people may be angry enough at violent juvenile offenders to believe that they deserve whatever horrors we force upon them. By regarding many youthful offenders

Clay Bennett, North America Syndicate. Used with permission.

as "inhuman," we give ourselves permission to treat them inhumanly. But demands for harsh, adult punishments of juveniles who commit "adult" crimes are often made in the name of self-defense, and as pragmatic, protective measures, they are bound to fail. You don't have to be an expert in criminal justice policy to understand that a teenager who is brutalized in prison will probably not metamorphose into a productive, law-abiding citizen, assuming he survives the experience.

Violence Begets Violence

By what process of rationalization might a society virtually obsessed with child abuse knowingly consign many of its children to hell? Of course, a minority have committed these dreadful crimes; they've earned a period of incarceration. But how can we assume that, at 14 or 15 years old, they are already beyond redemption?

Growing Up in Prison

The juvenile who is sentenced as an adult is not able to experience the responsibility and training for their adult life that the adults in prison experienced and that their nondelinquent peers get to experience. I must say though that there is a role for incarceration in juvenile justice. But putting juveniles into adult prisons denies them the developmental aid they still need and dooms them to physical and sexual assault far beyond the norm in juvenile facilities. That is why America quit doing it in the first place.

Gary LeRoux, *The Angolite*, March/April, 1999.

In David Kennedy's opinion, it is a great mistake to categorize all violent youthful offenders as hopelessly vicious and amoral. Kennedy, a senior researcher at Harvard's Kennedy School of Government, designed and directed the Boston Gun Project, an anti-violence initiative involving federal, state and local officials that has enjoyed dramatic success in reducing gang violence. "Not even gang members like being subjected to violence and many prefer not to commit violent acts," Kennedy observes. Like the cops, most of the kids involved in the Boston project wanted the violence to stop, but they needed help. "Kids get drawn into a self-sustaining dynamic of violence, and they can't get out of it alone."

Try Prevention, Not Punishment

Assuming that youth crime could be prevented, as well as punished, the Boston Gun Project offered the gangs a combination of incentives and disincentives to behave. Law enforcement officials made clear that violence would no longer be tolerated: Swift, comprehensive responses to gang violence proved the point. But gang members were also offered special services—assistance in getting high school diplomas or job training—and they were offered protection from other gangs, so that they would not act to protect themselves. Much of the violence stopped, and Kennedy stresses, "So far, it hasn't taken much to keep it stopped."

The Juvenile Crime Control Act provides no money for prevention programs, such as the Boston Gun Project, because it reflects no understanding of teenagers or teenage violence. It's based on a racist stereotype of sociopathic youthful predators. The Boston Gun Project is working partly because it assumes that even violent juveniles may be rational human beings, not compulsively violent, amoral offenders. Like most citizens, many juvenile offenders prefer peace and safety to violent disorder; they just need help achieving it.

> *"Parents who exhibit a reckless disregard for the potential criminal behavior of their kids likewise should be liable."*

Parents Should Be Held Legally Responsible for Juvenile Crime

Kate O'Beirne

By about 1960 most states had enacted some form of parental responsibility laws that typically require parents to pay penalties for minor property damage or personal injuries perpetrated by their children. In the following viewpoint, Kate O'Beirne claims that the current standard of parental liability is insufficient for many of today's violent juvenile crimes and should be strengthened accordingly. She believes that parents who fail to adequately monitor their children's behavior ought to be held legally responsible when those children commit crimes. O'Beirne is the Washington editor of the *National Review*, a conservative weekly magazine, as well as a contributing editor of *IntellectualCapital.com*, a weekly electronic public policy magazine.

As you read, consider the following questions:
1. What, according to O'Beirne, were three warning signs of violence displayed by Eric Harris?
2. As explained by the author, what kinds of criminal activity does current parental civil liability cover?
3. How, according to O'Beirne, could Harris' parents have been more involved?

Reprinted, with permission, from Kate O'Beirne, "Pro and Con: Can Bad Parenting Be a Crime?" *IntellectualCapital.com*, May 6, 1999.

Eric Harris and Dylan Klebold have been laid to rest following their shooting rampage through Columbine High, but their parents are being autopsied.

The two teenagers certainly seem to have broadcast their murderous intentions. Harris posted his violent rantings on the Web and turned his suburban home into a bomb factory. The barrel of a sawed-off shotgun sat on his dresser. In writing class, the gunmen penned essays that defended killing people, and they submitted a video for another class that depicted them roaming the halls, killing the school's athletes. They struck a shooting pose for a group photo in the yearbook.

The boys' parents were not the only adults who ignored the red flags in plain view, but they are seen as bearing the lion's share of the blame for their sons' assault.

Can Parenting Be a Crime?

That has led to a larger policy debate: When should parents be held criminally liable for the actions of their children? Colorado GOP Gov. Bill Owens' declaration that the evidence indicated the Harris and Klebold parents should be charged no doubt reflected the local sentiment in favor of criminal culpability. The rage and frustration that causes families to place responsibility on these parents is understandable. And parents should, in some cases, be held criminally liable for the actions of their children.

The issue of parents' civil liability is straightforward. Generally, parents are liable for the actions of their minor children that harm others. In Colorado, parents are strictly liable, but damages are strictly limited. Families of those killed or injured can sue for damages up to only $1,500, plus court costs and attorneys' fees. The state Legislature seemingly anticipated neighbors' windows broken by errant baseballs, or cars scratched by erratic bike riding—not felony violence. The law covers accidents that happen both among the most attentive families and the kind of inattention that makes some kids the scourge of their neighborhoods.

But surely the law should go further. Shouldn't parents who are criminally negligent in supervising their children be held criminally responsible? When a drunk driver kills, it matters not that he did not intend to take a life. In getting behind the wheel, he exhibited such a reckless disregard for others that he will be held criminally accountable. Parents who exhibit a reckless disregard for the potential criminal behavior of their kids likewise should be liable.

Were They More than Inattentive?

It is not clear to me that the parents of Littleton's triggermen were criminally negligent in the supervision of their sons. Friends of the Harris parents insist that they were involved, concerned parents who must have been totally unaware of Eric's evil designs. They were not involved enough to monitor their son's school assignments or Web activity, and they appear to have been inattentive to the bomb-making going on in their own home. They are now living with the heart-breaking consequences of their inattention.

Parents Are Responsible for Their Children

Parents are responsible for many things in the life of a child. A parent must consent before most medical procedures are performed on a child. Parents can be held financially liable for the actions of their children. Logically, therefore, parents should be held liable for the criminal actions of their children.

Oregon Daily Emerald, Nonline.com, April 26, 1997.

The simple negligence of both families is apparent. Parents are supposed to be nosy. We have an obligation to monitor our children as closely as possible. Harris had a swastika on his car. His parents should have demanded that he remove it. He was perfectly open with teachers about his violent fantasies. Was he completely circumspect in the presence of his parents?

Involved parents do not leave teenagers alone for hours and hours to engage in their nihilistic designs. The family garage typically is not an adult-free zone that allows for the construction of 30 pipe bombs. However, I would only support criminal accountability in the face of a higher standard of negligence.

I do not believe parents should be liable for simply having raised twisted offspring. For all we know, the parents of Ted

Bundy and Jeffrey Dahmer were caring and diligent. But parents should be criminally liable for the murderous acts of minor children who live at home when there is evidence of evil intent under their noses.

Eventually, we will no doubt learn the relevant details about life in the Harris and Klebold homes. If it is shown that the families had specific knowledge about the arsenals their sons were collecting, they should face criminal charges. Owners of vicious pit bulls should not face greater criminal accountability than parents who harbor murderous teens.

| "*When laws become an expression of frustration or an exercise in symbolism, they usually intensify the problem.*"

Holding Parents Legally Responsible for Juvenile Crime May Be Counterproductive

Garry Cooper

In 1994, Michigan passed a parental liability act holding parents legally accountable if their children committed such crimes as truancy, destruction of property, theft, or drug trafficking. Some critics contend that such laws only strain family relations and misplace blame on overwhelmed, confused parents instead of the adolescents committing the crimes. In the following viewpoint, Garry Cooper makes this argument by describing the case of the Provenzinos, whose son was caught harboring stolen property, weapons, and drugs in his parents' house. Cooper is a contributing editor for the *Family Therapy Networker*, a monthly mental health magazine.

As you read, consider the following questions:
1. Why did the judge give the Provenzinos the maximum punishment allowed by the parental responsibility law in Michigan?
2. What does Tony Jurich allege is a viable alternative to prosecuting parents for their children's crimes, as cited by the author?
3. Why, according to Jurich, do parental responsibility laws exacerbate, rather than alleviate, the actual cause of the delinquency?

Reprinted, with permission, from "Making Parents Responsible," by Garry Cooper, *Networker*, September/October 1996.

After 16-year-old Alex Provenzino, from an affluent Detroit suburban family, was sentenced to a year in prison for breaking and entering, the law went after his parents. It's not as if Anthony and Susan Provenzino hadn't been warned. Five months earlier, when Alex was arrested for burglary and marijuana violations, the court released him with an admonition to his parents to do a better job of supervising him. But when the police showed up at the Provenzino's home to question Alex about some new home and church burglaries, they found not only the stolen goods, but a handgun, knife, marijuana plant and alcohol, all in plain view in Alex's bedroom.

As a result, in May 1999, Alex's parents were charged and convicted under a local two-year-old parental responsibility ordinance, which allows prosecution of parents whose children violate curfew, repeatedly skip school, destroy property, hang out with juvenile delinquents or possess illegal drugs, guns or stolen property. Perhaps because Alex and his bedroom stash managed to score nearly 100 percent on the law's list of infractions, and certainly because the Provenzinos had already been warned to keep Alex under supervision, the judge gave the parents the maximum sentence: fines of $100 each and $1,000 in court costs. He did not hit them with the $27,000 in damages caused by Alex's burglaries, only because he felt that part of the parental responsibility law was in conflict with another state law, and judges hate to be overturned on appeal. Michigan weather notwithstanding, the Provenzinos are lucky they don't live in California, one of 10 states (and dozens of communities) with parental responsibility laws with a maximum sentence of a year in jail and a $250 fine, or five years probation.

Address Causes Not Symptoms

As America continues to get tougher on crime, the old conception of the juvenile justice system—as a separate and distinct system designed to protect and rehabilitate rather than punish an immature, impulsive youngster—is under assault. Rep. Bill McCollum (R-Fla.), chairman of the House Crime Subcommittee, warning Americans to "brace [themselves] for the coming generation of super-predators," has recently introduced a bill that would end the federal mandates that require states to segregate juveniles from adults in jails and prisons. More juveniles are being prosecuted as adults. Sentencing guidelines have become harsher. The once-sacrosanct confidentiality of juvenile court proceedings is being eroded—only 22 states and the District of Columbia exclude the public from most juvenile court hearings. Seen from the get-tough perspective, parental responsibility laws are an attempt to add another deterrent: not only are the kids getting stiffer punishments, but their parents are going to pay as well. No doubt inspired by the local St. Claire Shores, Michigan, ordinance, a statewide parental responsibility bill is now being debated in the Michigan state legislature.

Parents Need Help, Not Punishment

An emphasis on fining parents [for their children's crimes] is likely to produce injustice, to place struggling families under even greater stress and to increase rather than reduce the problems which promote delinquency. The Penal Affairs Consortium considers that constructive programs designed to support families under stress and to help parents exercise parental responsibility more effectively will do much more to reduce youth crime than such punitive approaches.

Panel Affairs Consortium, Nonline.com, April 26, 1997.

But laws work best when they address causes instead of symptoms. When laws become an expression of frustration or an exercise in symbolism, they usually intensify the problem. The reality in America today is that many parents are exhausted, their financial and emotional resources are strained and society gives them little nurturing or support. Most therapists would argue that adolescents' problems are not caused by parents suddenly deciding not to exercise responsibility, and that parents need help, not additional stigmatization and punishment. Instead of putting the state's time and money into prosecuting parents, why not provide classes in parenting for prospective parents and make family therapy more easily accessible, asks Tony Jurich, president-elect of the American Association for Marriage and Family Therapy (AAMFT) and professor of Family Studies and Human Services at Kansas State University.

The picture of Anthony and Susan Provenzino that emerges from the trial is not one of unconcerned or lazy parents, but one of confused, frightened people. When Anthony tried to confront Alex about his behavior, Alex swung a golf club at his father's head. In dealing with their son, the Provenzinos felt they were in over their heads; nothing they tried seemed to work with Alex (who, incidentally, is one of four children). It might be argued that a child such as Alex is a result of years of poor parenting, but the question remains whether well-intentioned but poor parenting ought to be grounds for prosecution.

Effects on the Family

Some family therapists have been critical of parental responsibility laws. fearing that they may ultimately accomplish the opposite of what's intended. The problem doesn't get fixed, and in fact such laws may actually exacerbate the very causes of the problem. "You have to look at the real message parental responsibility laws are giving," says Jurich. "Instead of helping the parents take responsibility, which we absolutely have to do in many cases, we're punishing them for not doing it. Guess what? Getting punished still doesn't mean you've taken responsibility. Plus, by implying that the parents are to blame for what the kid has done, you're reinforcing the message to the kid that he isn't really responsible for what he's done. Suddenly it's the parents' fault."

Some therapists do see a limited usefulness in parental responsibility laws. Jerry Price, a family therapist who works near Detroit, insists, "There has to be a hierarchy in the family. Parents need to be in charge and kids, short of being abused, need to do what parents tell them. If parental responsibility laws help give some parents enough backbone to stand up to their kids, the laws are a good thing." In Price's view, ineffectual or depressed parents who lack enough self-esteem to take a stand may find it easier to be assertive because of a law—not unlike clients in therapy who temporarily borrow the therapist's ego.

Another beneficial effect of such laws, says Price, is to make parents so uncomfortable that "instead of doing nothing and ultimately paying a heavy price, they can find another solution, hopefully earlier, that works better. For example, they might decide it's cheaper to pay for family therapy than for fines and court costs. By pushing people to choose; the law can be ultimately empowering." But Price is careful to point out that to be effective, the laws must be applied selectively—in cases where they are likely to motivate rather than punish. In the present punitive and politically charged atmosphere surrounding juvenile crime, however, it is unlikely that most judges will ponder such distinctions.

Increasingly, as more communities and states enact parental responsibility laws, the courts are likely to find themselves in the same position as the parents they will be judging—right on the front lines of the fight to maintain stability and appropriate control, with a mandate that may sometimes be overwhelming. The question is: will the courts throw up their hands and explode in abusive punitiveness, or will they somehow be able to exercise the wisdom and restraint that we expect from both judges and parents?

> "*I never see groups of adults on the street till all hours, so why do kids need to be 'hanging out'? Being out late only increases your chances of getting into trouble.*"

Curfew Laws Are Effective at Combating Juvenile Crime

David Knight

Many communities have recently enacted curfew laws as a means of preventing juvenile crime. In the following viewpoint, David Knight argues that curfew laws can be an effective aid in controlling teenagers. He maintains that being out late increases the risk of teenage drinking and fighting. Curfews can reduce these risks by ensuring that minors are off the streets and not involved in criminal activity. Knight is a parent who began his career as a deputy sheriff in 1984.

As you read, consider the following questions:

1. What, according to Knight, are three facts of teenage curfew laws?
2. What are two reasons Knight cites for curfew laws?
3. How, in Knight's opinion, can curfew laws help parents better control their children?

Reprinted, with permission, from David Knight, "The Curfew Myth," *Parenting Today's Teen*, September 1, 1996.

As parents, we look forward to the time when our kids are old enough to watch after themselves, drive themselves to school, the store or the beach. We look forward to having some private time for ourselves, right? But to do this, we must rely heavily on our kids. We must trust them to be alone, or to be where they claim they are, or even to come home on time. We rely on them to tell us the truth.

Unfortunately, what we often get from our kids is not truth; it is myth. "No!" you may say, "My kid would never lie!" It's easier for some parents to believe their son really did plan on going to "Johnny's" house, even though Johnny "wasn't home," or maybe there really isn't a Johnny. Or they didn't go to the beach because it was "just too crowded!" Here's a new one: "What?" they say, quite astounded, "Do you mean to tell me that Tijuana isn't in the United States? No way!" As a parent, you've heard it all, and more, but although you may not always have control over where they are, or what they' re doing, there is one area that you should not only be aware of, but be in complete control over: Curfew.

Facts About Curfew Laws

Your kids will tell you that curfew is midnight or 2 A.M., or maybe that there isn't one. Or better yet, that they can stay out all night as long as they are with someone 18 years or older. It's all a myth.

Well, here are the facts:

1. Is there a curfew? Yes, most communities have had a curfew for years, and most curfew laws are very clear-cut. According to the Justice Department, 146 of America's 200 largest cities have curfew laws.

2. What ages are affected by curfew? Anyone under the age of 18 years, except for someone who is emancipated.

3. Are there exceptions to curfew? Of course! They would include the following:

a. Curfew does not apply when the minor is with a parent or legal guardian;

b. Or when traveling directly home from a school, work or church function;

c. Or when sent on an emergency.

4. Can a parent give their child an extended curfew? No.

A parent cannot change the law, in fact, it is against the law to allow your child to stay out after curfew; you can be fined.

5. Are there punishments for violating curfew? Yes. For example, in San Diego, it is a misdemeanor to violate curfew. In San Diego, a first offense is a $20 to $27 fine and attendance at a 3-hour curfew program at an additional cost of $20. A second offense jumps up to a $135 fine, and the court then can start restricting the child's drivers license, even if they do not have one. (The driver's license restrictions may mean a loss of driving privileges for several months to several years. If your child does not have a license yet, the court may put off the time the child can receive one. I have seen this punishment work very effectively.)

Why Have a Curfew?

Communities found that parents were not effective enough when it came to keeping young people off the streets late at night. Communities also found that establishing a curfew helped curtail youth violence, although many critics will argue that teens can get into trouble just as easily before curfew. True, yet curfew for the young helps to control those in whom there is little self-control.

Curfews Are Useful and Cost-Effective

"Curfews—both day and night—continue to be a growing trend in the United States as city officials look for answers to ensure the safety and youth in their communities," said National League of Cities (NLC) President Bob Knight, mayor of Wichita, Kansas. "The findings [of a poll of 490 cities] show that cities have a confidence in their usefulness and find them cost-effective, as well."

National League of Cities, February 28, 2000.

In my opinion, there is no need to be out late on a school night, for the same reason I don't stay out late if I have to be at work the following morning. And even on non-school nights, what purpose is there to be out on the streets at midnight? What is there to do? [Working patrol late at night, I never see groups of adults on the street till all hours, so why do kids need to be "hanging out"? Being out late only increases your chances of getting into trouble.]

As a cop, I can tell you from experience that when a group of kids get together late at night, bad things tend to happen. Alcohol, drugs, sex and fighting all seem to creep into the mix; alcohol seems to be the primary abuse. I'm not saying that a group of kids can't get together at someone's home or even go to the movies in the evening, but peer pressure is on them in a big way and self-control, overall, usually is lacking.

Help for Parents

Now, I know not every kid who stays out after curfew is going to get into trouble. Most kids I've ever arrested for curfew got into trouble because someone called to complain about a loud party or kids drinking alcohol. I've always wondered why kids complain and ask, "Why are you picking on me?" as they crank their stereos all the way up, drink beer and holler at the top of their lungs. Common sense and responsibility are the key factors for anyone, adult or juvenile, being out in public.

Despite the arguments against it, curfew laws do help you in controlling your child. Any time you can defer a rule to someone or something other than yourself, it helps you a great deal in dealing with your kids. After all, you don't make the rules or laws, you are not the only parent in the world with rules, and you certainly don't make this stuff up. You just have to help your kids toe the line. And now, curfew isn't a myth anymore. If you would like the curfew time for your area, contact your local police department.

"Curfews are the hemophiliac's Band-Aid."

Curfew Laws Are Ineffective at Combating Juvenile Crime

Colin Miller

In an effort to reduce juvenile crime, authorities in many cities have utilized curfew laws, making it illegal for minors to be outside their homes or school during designated hours. Opponents claim that curfew laws are unconstitutional and a waste of police time and taxpayers' money. Colin Miller makes this argument in the following viewpoint, suggesting that alternatives such as after-school programs may be more effective than curfews at deterring crime. Miller is a columnist for the *Cavalier Daily*, an independent daily newspaper at the University of Virginia.

As you read, consider the following questions:
1. What does Miller claim are three problems with curfew laws?
2. What does Miller consider the greatest cost of a curfew?
3. What, according to the author, does the Fairfax County solution reveal as two essential ingredients in combating teenage crime?

Reprinted, with permission, from Colin Miller, "Curfew Laws Curb Rights," *The Cavalier Daily*, December 4, 1997.

We are justified in panicking at the amebic expansion in juvenile crime. A study by the organization Fight Crime: Invest in Kids reveals that teenage killing exploded by 141 percent from 1985 to 1995. Our soundbyte politicians, following Bill Clinton's 'lead,' have implemented curfews across the country, including in Charlottesville, as the solution. A U.S. Conference of Mayors survey found that 90 percent of officials in cities with curfews believed "enforcing them was a good use of police officer's time." In reality, however, curfew laws are unconstitutional, misguided and ineffective.

In May 1997, U.S. District Judge James Michael Jr. upheld Charlottesville's curfew law as the "least restrictive means possible" to prevent adolescent crime. He was wrong. First, city curfews infringe upon the rights of parents to raise their children. The Court of Appeals in Washington struck down a curfew law on this very ground, holding that such laws "prohibit parents from allowing their children to participate in beneficial programs or groups which may keep them out after curfew hours." The biggest slap in the face for these parents is that they can be fined when their children are caught out after curfew. In effect, then, curfews take away the right of parents to raise their children and concurrently increase the responsibility parents have for their children's actions.

Problems with Curfew Laws

At the same time, curfew laws infringe on an adolescent's freedom of movement and expression protected under the First Amendment. Curfews fallaciously criminalize even constructive, law-abiding behavior by adolescents who happen to be out late. Clearly, there are less restrictive alternatives like only applying curfews to designated dangerous areas and to juvenile delinquents.

Furthermore, curfew laws are severely misguided. Curfews usually prohibit minors from public areas from 11 P.M. until 7 A.M. Newer day curfews during school hours also have been implemented to prevent truancy and delinquency. Unfortunately, these hours of the day are when the least amount of juvenile crime occurs. Statistics from FBI reports in eight states reveal that almost two-thirds of all juvenile crime takes place between 2 P.M. and 11 P.M. After 8 P.M., crime substantially drops and becomes almost negligible after 11 P.M. Finally, only one-seventh of violent juvenile crime—murders, rapes, robberies and aggravated assaults—occurs during the curfew hours of 11 P.M. to 7 A.M.

Curfews Are Unjust

Curfew laws do adolescents a great injustice by punishing the many for the faults of the few.

Curfews simply are not an adequate solution for teenage crime. Perhaps a more effective option would be creating teen centers and youth programs that would give teenagers an enjoyable way to spend their time off the streets.

Amy Tay, *Los Angeles Times*, February 8, 1998.

Thus, curfews only potentially affect the periphery of juvenile crime, and with great cost. San Jose estimates that curfew enforcement has led to a $1 million raise in police payroll costs. New Orleans officials complain that curfew laws lead to increased overtime pay for officers. Arizona officials point to significant costs and backlog associated with more adolescent court appearances. The greatest cost of a curfew, however, is when police are deterred from preventing pernicious crimes while detaining star-gazing teenagers at night.

Alternative Solutions

My argument is not that we should decrease efforts or finances to combat juvenile crime. If anything, we should be more committed than ever. I'm also not claiming the streets are safe at night or that all juveniles are always out late with only humanitarian or capricious intentions. Clearly, many adolescents are out late to scar property and rivals. But curfews are the hemophiliac's Band-Aid.

In September 1997, Fairfax County, Virginia, decided against curfews, holding them to be inefficient and ineffective. First, the county held that curfews place substantial new burdens on police officers at hours when juvenile crime is, at most, sporadic. In addition, curfews are merely reactionary and superficial. They attempt to reduce crime by prohibiting any juveniles from being out late rather than attempting to address and prevent the causes of teenage crime.

Instead, Fairfax County decided to create a task force to study how to address the rise in teenage crime. The task force has advanced such initiatives as an agency to coordinate services provided by local organizations, enhanced funding and supervision of drug-abuse programs and increasing adult-supervised after-school activities. Task force member Howard Perlstein correctly claims "the solution is much more complex than arresting and prosecuting . . . youths off the street who have violated the law. It is addressing why youths act violently and [how should] society . . . address the causes."

The Fairfax County solution reveals two essential ingredients in combating teenage crime. First, we must attempt to address the causes of delinquency instead of merely denying rights to adolescents. Adolescence is a time for young citizens to become adults and only by affording minors rights and respect can we foster growth. Second, we need to divert funds from curfews to after-school programs. Increases in teenage crime are directly correlated to community cutbacks in after-school programs. Logically, because most teenage crime occurs in the hours after school, solutions addressing these hours have the best potential to reduce crime.

Advocating curfews may be politically advantageous for politicians and may make us feel good, but we need substantive solutions to address such a complex problem as teenage crime. Let's follow Fairfax County's lead and reject curfews across the country.

"Simple logic suggests that violent young offenders who presently suffer little or no incarceration ought to be held for far longer terms."

Harsher Punishment Is the Answer to Juvenile Crime

Peter Reinhartz

In 1899 the juvenile justice system was formed to focus on rehabilitation instead of punishment in an effort to create productive citizens out of delinquents. Juveniles generally receive lighter punishments than adults, and their records are sealed when they reach eighteen, although the specifics vary from state to state. Opponents of the juvenile justice system argue that it encourages juvenile delinquency by failing to hold youths responsible for their crimes. Peter Reinhartz makes this argument in the following viewpoint, focusing specifically on the existing juvenile justice system in New York. Reinhartz is a prosecuting attorney with the New York juvenile justice department.

As you read, consider the following questions:
1. According to Reinhartz, what is one of the limitations on police in the juvenile justice system?
2. What does Reinhartz consider to be two advantages conferred by Youthful Offender status?
3. What, in the author's opinion, is the principal purpose of the juvenile justice system?

Reprinted, with permission, from Peter Reinhartz, "Why Teen Thugs Get Away with Murder," *City Journal*, Autumn 1996.

Everything in the juvenile justice system is designed to relieve teen malefactors of responsibility for their criminal acts. Under the Family Court Act [which governs the administration of juvenile justice in New York], gun-toting teen muggers are not criminals but juvenile "delinquents," and they have not committed crimes but rather "acts which if committed by an adult would be a crime." As they haven't committed crimes, it follows that they acquire no criminal record. They are charged in Family Court as "respondents," not as defendants. They are not indicted but "charged in a petition." They don't go to trial but appear at a "fact-finding hearing," where they are "adjudicated" rather than convicted, and they go to "disposition" rather than being sentenced. For a felony assault that results in a mangled face and a punctured eye, the architects of New York's juvenile justice system do not want to punish the offender; they seek his rehabilitation through treatment.

But first you have to catch a teen criminal—and the Family Court Act makes that even harder to do than catching adult criminals. The Family Court has no power to issue search warrants. The only way within New York's present juvenile justice system to enter an apartment to retrieve, say, a gun brandished by a 15-year-old mugger is to rely on the good faith of the perpetrator or the cooperation and consent of one of his parents. If the police do retrieve the gun without a search warrant, lawyers for the offender—usually from New York City's largest criminal defense office, the Legal Aid Society—would seek suppression of the weapon as evidence on the grounds that police acted outside the Constitution, which requires a search warrant. Of course, the Legal Aid Society has repeatedly opposed giving the Family Court the authority to issue search warrants, assuring their armed clients the protection of a legal Catch-22: no search warrant authority for the court, but an absolute requirement for a search warrant in order to seize evidence without fear of suppression. . . .

Youthful Offender Protection

New York, it is often said, is tough on teen criminals: after all, once they turn 16, it tries them not in Family Court but in the adult criminal courts. Many other states don't send them to adult courts until they reach 17 or 18. New York even sends 14- and 15-year-olds to the adult courts for rape or armed robbery or for an assault with a deadly weapon that leaves the victim crippled for life. This toughness, though, is usually mere illusion. For New York has still another cloak of protection to throw over these criminals: the Youthful Offender (YO) law.

A judge can choose to grant YO status to a teen thug at the time of sentencing, and the promise of it is often part of a plea bargain in felonies involving 16-, 17-, and 18-year-old defendants (along with 14- and 15-year-old offenders tried in adult court). YO status confers several advantages. First, it automatically reduces the sentence the offender faces— from a maximum of 5 to 15 years for a second-degree robbery, say, to a mere 1⅓ to 4 years. In practice, however, most YOs get nothing more than 5 years of probation—an even lighter sentence than the paltry 18 months they might have gotten in Family Court.

Second, this section of the Criminal Procedure Law allows the courts to transform a criminal conviction into a non-criminal adjudication. All criminal aspects of the case—including the criminal record—disappear, in the hope that the offender's misdeed was an isolated error of youth. The case record is sealed and remains unavailable for public inspection or even for use in future sentencing. Result: if a violent YO robber, free on probation, commits another violent robbery, the court must consider him a first-time offender. So instead of facing a much stiffer penalty as a second-time felony robber, he will just be sentenced as an adult first-timer. . . .

The philosophy behind the state's no-fault juvenile justice system might have made sense in the days when juvenile offenders stole apples and picked pockets, often driven by poverty. Such acts really might have been isolated errors of youth, so the law gave these kids another chance, saving them from the lifelong stigma of their isolated mistakes and treating them not as criminals but as children in need of the paternal care of the state. But are the teen criminals in court today, almost nine out of ten of whom are violent felons, really juvenile delinquents rather than criminals?

Failure of Rehabilitation

Does it make sense to think in such terms about chronic malefactors like Keith A., who was prosecuted along with several accomplices for savagely beating a drunk in upper Manhattan's Mount Morris Park and then dousing him with lighter fluid, as he screamed and begged, and burning him so badly that his charred corpse was scarcely recognizable? Keith, a couple of weeks shy of his 13th birthday (though a burly 15-year-old in appearance), then went home and had a snack: indifference to human life doesn't come much more depraved. Keith's neighbors knew he was trouble and crossed the street to avoid him; he'd beaten up drunks before, with bloodthirsty zeal, and he was on probation for grabbing and groping a girl at a swimming pool. Does it make sense to think that the 18-month sentence he received for the murder will bring him to his senses and set him on the straight and narrow?

Cracking Down on Youth Offenders

The current system obviously is not working. Barely a day goes by when there is not an article in a newspaper or segment on the television news concerning some violent juvenile crime. Juveniles are engaging in gang wars, raping old women, holding up convenience stores and shooting police officers. Simply offering more variations of cushy rehabilitation programs for the youth is not going to work. Instead, we need to crack down on crime. We need harsher punishment and stricter rehabilitation programs.

Robin Pinnel, *Cavalier Daily*, January 19, 1996.

And what about the fundamental assumption that underlies the whole philosophy of New York's juvenile justice system—the idea that the system's principal purpose is rehabilitation? Is there the ghost of a chance that the 36-month sentence handed out to 15-year-old Stacy L. will send him back to society rehabilitated? Two 13-year-old boys were walking together one morning near Lincoln Center when one of them accidentally bumped into Stacy. Both kept walking when he demanded an apology. Enraged, he spat out a few anti-white epithets and then kicked and stomped the two boys, knocking one unconscious and severing the ligaments in the other's wrist, so that even after many operations he will never regain full use of it. The unconscious boy was left with blurred vision and memory loss. But as Stacy told the court psychologist, he "likes to hurt people." Fond of guns, which he often carries, he had a robbery charge pending at the time of the attack. The psychologist concluded that he had an explosive personality, with a tendency toward violence, and ought to be removed from the community. But Stacy will almost certainly be back in our midst in about two years—bigger, stronger, unrehabilitated.

The truth is, we have had very little success rehabilitating violent teens. We've tried counseling and family preservation, prevention programs and community-based services—all with no discernible result. Boot camps, the most promising recent rehabilitation scheme, have just been shown to be a failure by a National Institute of Justice study. All the programs in the study exhibited "high attrition rates for non-compliance, absenteeism, and new arrests." Even during their time in boot camp, offenders committed assaults against inmates and staff; some escaped. Those offenders who graduated and went into a follow-up program were arrested at rates of up to 70 percent before they had even finished the program. . . .

Longer Incarceration Terms

Juvenile justice philosophy runs counter to the criminological data. [Simple logic suggests that violent young offenders who presently suffer little or no incarceration ought to be held for far longer terms.] What purpose is served by setting the periods of incarceration for armed juvenile felons at only a few months, or giving them probation in a YO plea deal, when the statistics tell us that they are likely to commit more, and worse, crimes when released? Were the juvenile courts to sentence them to terms of six or seven or eight years, the total amount of crime would drop precipitously. Even if juveniles had to spend three or four years in confinement between crimes, the total amount of crime would shrink drastically. The sad truth about the juvenile justice system in New York is that it does little to interfere with young criminal careers.

Not only has it largely done away with the best means of preventing crime—locking up criminals—but it also fails to send the message that society takes crime seriously enough to hold criminals responsible and punish them severely. In every way, it has blunted the natural consequences of criminal actions. Indeed, the architects of the juvenile justice process have worked hard to create a system and a euphemistic language that deflect individual responsibility and remove all stigma and shame from the process. But these powerful sentiments are society's best deterrent to antisocial behavior; virtually doing away with them ensures recidivism.

"Violent juvenile crime triples in the hour after school ends, and after-school hours are peak hours for kids to become crime victims or to be involved with drugs, alcohol, and sex."

More After-School Programs Are the Answer to Juvenile Crime

Judy Mann

Many critics of the juvenile justice system believe that prevention, rather than punishment, is the key to reducing juvenile crime. Proponents believe that early intervention programs can steer juveniles away from delinquency and reduce their chances of becoming hardened criminals. In the following viewpoint, Judy Mann emphasizes the importance of early intervention and after-school programs in preventing juvenile crime. She also describes the higher academic success rate of students involved in after-school and community programs compared with students who are not involved in such activities. Mann is a metro columnist with the *Washington Post*.

As you read, consider the following questions:
1. What does Mann describe as the bedrock philosophy of the Fight Crime: Invest in Kids organization?
2. What are three dimensions of the Invest-in-Kids plan?
3. How, according to Mann, does the Balanced Budget Act affect prevention and after-school programs?

Reprinted, with permission, from Judy Mann, "Invest in Kids Now, or Pay Later," *The Washington Post*, July 28, 1999, p. C15; © 1999 The Washington Post.

In an average week, 40 children are killed in America by violence. Most of these killings—98 percent, in fact—take place outside of schools. We are paralyzed with shock at the killings in a Littleton, Colo., high school, but do the math and it shows the deaths among youngsters that don't make the headlines add up to more than 150 Littletons a year.

In the last few months of 1999, there's been the usual hand wringing over school violence and the requisite White House conference. But at summer's midpoint, when policies and programs affecting schools should be moving into place for fall's opening, there's scant evidence of significant changes. In fact, programs that could prevent youth violence are in considerable jeopardy in the Republican tax-cutting plans. In the end, Littleton has not had much of an impact.

What makes this more than a pity, what makes it really unforgivable, is that there are proven programs that curb violence and other dangerous behavior.

Early Intervention

Fight Crime: Invest in Kids is an organization formed in 1996 with the bedrock philosophy memorably expressed by former Winston-Salem police chief George Sweat. As he put it: The fight against crime "needs to start in the highchair, not wait for the electric chair." What gives the message so much clout is that it comes from a group whose members include 500 police chiefs, sheriffs, district attorneys, violence prevention scholars, as well as parents who have lost children to violence. This is not the ivory tower liberal set. These are people who are on the bloody front lines.

They have put together a School and Youth Violence Prevention plan, which has been endorsed by many national and state law enforcement organizations. Minimizing access to guns is a given. But their plan also involves other aspects, including early intervention and prevention programs that spot troubled kids and make sure they get timely and effective help. Most young people who engage in violence show signs of problems in elementary school. Fight Crime: Invest in Kids cites studies that show that children who get professional help when they are young are 50 percent less likely to be delinquent later on.

They want all children to have access to good after-school programs. The importance of this can't be overstated: [Violent juvenile crime triples in the hour after school ends, and after-school hours are peak hours for kids to become crime victims or to be involved with drugs, alcohol or sex. Being unsupervised after school doubles the risk that eighth-graders will smoke, drink or use drugs.]

Getting the Family Involved

But there are programs that work against those influences. In a five-city study, half of a group of at-risk high school youngsters were assigned to participate in the Quantum Opportunities after-school program. The high school freshman boys randomly selected from welfare households were only one-sixth as likely to be convicted of a crime during the high school years as those not selected. All of the boys and girls selected were one-fourth as likely to be convicted of a crime as those not chosen. The boys and girls who participated in the program were 50 percent more likely to graduate from high school on time.

The third part of the invest-in-kids plan would provide access to early childhood development programs for all families.

Mike Thompson. Reprinted by permission of Copley News Service.

This is the time when children learn to get along with others. Researchers at the High/Scope Educational Research Foundation enrolled half a group of low-income toddlers in quality child care. Twenty-two years later, those left out were five times as likely to have become chronic lawbreakers.

After-School Programs Prevent Crime

The peak hours for juvenile crime (as with drug use, smoking and drinking and sex) are 3 p.m. to 6 p.m., according to the National Center for Juvenile Justice. A study of an intensive after-school program called Quantum Opportunities showed that the poor high school boys who participated [in the program] were one-sixth as likely to be convicted of a crime during high school as the kids left out of the program, according to the Center for the Study and Prevention of Violence.

Geneva Overholser, *Washington Post*, January 18, 2000.

The fourth dimension calls for preventing child abuse through programs that coach parents on how to relate to their children, and through programs to help heal abused and neglected youngsters. Parenting programs for low-income, first-time mothers have cut abuse and neglect by 80 percent and halved the numbers of subsequent pregnancies.

Budget Matters

Economist Steven Barnett found that the High/Scope Foundation's Perry Preschool program saved $150,000 per participant in costs that would have been incurred had they become involved in crime.

When Professor Mark A. Cohen, of Vanderbilt University, studied chronic offenders, he estimated that each youngster saved from a life of chronic crime saves Americans between $1.7 million and $2.3 million in the cost of incarceration and in victim costs, such as pain and suffering and property loss.

These kinds of programs should be expanded as part of a crime-fighting initiative. Instead, they are going to be put on life support if the tax cut package approved by the House becomes law.

There is, as with all budget matters, some history. When

Congress adopted the Balanced Budget Act in 1997 it required massive, across-the-board spending cuts, starting with small cuts in fiscal 1997 and 1998. Cuts of 11 percent to 14 percent are required [in 1999], with more cuts over the next 10 years. The budget surplus we've been hearing so much about is dependent on these spending caps.

Sanford A. Newman, president of Fight Crime: Invest in Kids, says, "Key Republicans who head the appropriation process have already said they can't even come up with appropriations bills that stay within these caps, so it's been widely assumed they'd be lifted this year since cuts are no longer necessary to balance the budget. These bills would lock in massive budget cuts and likely produce a massive crime wave for decades to come."

These spending caps have gotten relatively little attention, but their implications for federal spending in all areas, including law enforcement and programs for children, are huge. Instead of investing in kids, we are headed straight down the road of investing in criminals. It's shortsighted and fiscally foolish. It makes even less sense if you allow yourself to think about the heartache and human tragedy of children lost to violence.

Periodical Bibliography

The following articles have been selected to supplement the diverse views presented in this chapter. Addresses are provided for periodicals not indexed in the *Readers' Guide to Periodical Literature*, the *Alternative Press Index*, the *Social Sciences Index*, or the *Index to Legal Periodicals and Books*.

Vikas Bajaj	"Locking Up Juveniles for Life Not the Answer," *State News*, April 1, 1998. Available from 343 Student Services, East Lansing, MI 48824.
Michael Bochenek	"United States Must Do Part to Stop Executions of Juvenile Criminals," *Atlantic Journal-Constitution*, August 22, 2000. Available from PO Box 4689, Atlanta, GA 30302.
Jeffrey Butts and Adele Harrell	"One-Size-Fits-All Justice Simply Isn't Fair, Should the Punishment Fit the Crime or Fit the Offender? Trying Kids as Adults is a 'Get-Tough' Overreaction," *Christian Science Monitor*, December 1, 1998.
Delbert S. Elliott	"Put Greater Focus on Prevention," *USA Today*, June 21, 1999.
T. Markus Funk	"Adult Treatment Fits 'Predators,'" *San Francisco Chronicle*, July 7, 1997. Available from 901 Mission St., San Francisco, CA 94103.
Dave Grossman	"Teaching Kids to Kill," *Phi Kappa Phi Journal*, Fall 2000. Available from PO Box 16000, Louisiana State University, Baton Rouge, LA 70893.
Darlene Kennedy	"Let's Hold Juveniles Responsible for Their Crimes," *National Policy Analysis*, August 1997. Available from the National Center for Public Policy Research, 777 N. Capitol St. NE, Suite 803, Washington, DC 20002.
Charles Levandosky	"House Passes Its Own Abominable Juvenile Crime Bill," *Liberal Opinion Week*, August 9, 1999. Available from 421 1st Ave. Vinton, IA 52349.
Newsday	"Not Just Kid Stuff," *Newsday*, July 24, 1994. Available from 235 Pinelawn Rd., Melville, NY 11747.
Robyn Nordell	"Curfew Laws Violate Our Constitutional Rights," *Orange County Register*, January 7, 1998. Available from PO Box 11944, Santa Ana, CA 92711.

Geneva Overholser — "Tough on Crime, Care for Kids," *Washington Post*, January 18, 2000. Available from 1150 15th St. NW, Washington, DC 20071.

William S. Pollack — "The Columbine Syndrome," *National Forum*, Fall 2000. Available from 4000 Lock Ln., Suite 9/KL, Lake Charles, LA 70605.

Amy Tay — "Curfew Today, Bedtime Tomorrow?" *Los Angeles Times*, February 8, 1998. Available from Times Mirror Square, Los Angeles, CA 90053.

Walter E. Williams — "Making a Case for Corporal Punishment," *Insight*, September 13, 1999. Available from PO Box 91022, Washington, DC 20090.

Jason Ziedenberg and Vincent Schiraldi — "The Risks Juveniles Face," *Corrections Today*, August 1998.

For Further Discussion

Chapter 1

1. Steve Macko and James Glassman describe horrific incidents of violent crime committed by juveniles. Macko claims that these incidents portend a coming surge of violent crime, while Glassman argues that they are extremely rare and isolated occurrences. What evidence does each author present to support his conclusion? Whose use of evidence is most persuasive? Explain your answer.

2. The National Center for Victims of Crime contends that recent incidents of school shootings, the threat of gangs, and the presence of drugs contribute to a major problem of juvenile crime in schools. Patrick Welsh argues that rare incidents of crime have made schools seem to be less safe that they actually are. How does each viewpoint compare to your own experiences at school? Whose argument do you find most realistic? Explain.

3. Scott Minerbrook contends that child abuse, poverty, and the threat of street gangs are turning children into cold-blooded killers. Ira Glasser argues that the media exaggerate incidents of juvenile crime and distort public perception of its severity. Whose argument do you find most convincing, and why?

Chapter 2

1. Sharon Begley and Tom O'Connor both contend that child abuse is a contributing factor to juvenile crime. Begley maintains, however, that a particular biology must be present for the abuse to turn the child into a criminal. Evaluate each author's opinion and formulate your own argument on the causes of juvenile crime, citing from the texts.

2. Richard Rhodes argues that children learn violent behavior from abusive family members or peers, while Dave Grossman contends that the violence on television and in the news encourages "cluster murders." Whose argument do you agree with more? Whose use of evidence do you find most effective, and why?

3. Bob Levin claims that such tragedies as school shootings could not have occurred without the access juveniles have to guns. But, as Timothy Wheeler articulates, Americans have the constitutional right to protect themselves with their own firearms. Do you think that it is necessary for Americans to own their own guns? Do you think that access to guns enables children to commit violent acts? Explain your answer.

4. Mike Males contends that the root cause of juvenile crime and violence is poverty, while Dave Kopel claims that an epidemic of fatherless homes leads children into a life of crime. What do you think the relationship is between poverty and fatherless families? Construct an argument that combines both Males' and Kopel's arguments, citing from the texts.

Chapter 3

1. Suren Pillay argues that entertainment industries contribute to gang-related juvenile crime by marketing gang-associated styles to young people. Do you agree with his argument? Can you think of any popular companies that use gang-related trends to sell their products?

2. This chapter discusses various viewpoints on the causes of gang-related juvenile crime. Which do you think are the most important, and why? Can you think of any other factors that contribute to gang involvement?

3. In Paul Palango's viewpoint, Kathleen claims to have been influenced by the violent lyrics of rap music. Do you think that the lyrics in rap music can be a negative influence on a teenager, or is rap a harmless form of entertainment? Explain your answer.

4. Christian Smith describes the court ordered injunctions against the 18th Street gang as unconstitutional and discriminatory. Do you agree with his assessment? Do you think the court's decision is in the public's best interest? Explain.

Chapter 4

1. Hanna Chiou argues that teenagers are mature enough to distinguish right from wrong and should suffer adult punishments if they commit adult crimes. Wendy Kaminer maintains that juveniles incarcerated with adults emerge even more brutal and crime-prone than they were before going to jail. Whose argument do you find most convincing, and why?

2. Garry Cooper describes the case of the Provenzinos, who were forced to pay fines under a Michigan law holding parents legally responsible for their children's crimes. Do you think that this is a just law? Citing from both Cooper's and Kate O'Beirne's viewpoints, explain why you think the law is or is not fair.

3. David Knight claims that curfews are an effective tool against juvenile delinquency, while Colin Miller argues that curfew laws are unconstitutional and waste valuable police time and effort. Whose use of evidence do you find most persuasive, and why?

4. Peter Reinhartz argues that the increasing severity of teenage crime necessitates harsher punishments than the current juvenile justice system provides. Judy Mann claims that prevention, rather than punishment, is the best method of curbing juvenile crime. Using arguments from both viewpoints, how do you think juvenile crime can best be combated?

Organizations to Contact

The editors have compiled the following list of organizations concerned with the issues debated in this book. The descriptions are derived from materials provided by the organizations. All have publications or information available for interested readers. The list was compiled on the date of publication of the present volume; the information provided here may change. Be aware that many organizations take several weeks or longer to respond to inquiries, so allow as much time as possible.

ABA Juvenile Justice Center
740 15th St. NW, Washington, DC 20005
(202) 662-1506 • fax: (202) 662-1501
e-mail: juvjus@abanet.org
website: www.abanet.org/crimjust/juvjust/home.html

An organization of the American Bar Association, the Juvenile Justice Center disseminates information on juvenile justice systems across the country. The center provides leadership to state and local practitioners, bar associations, judges, youth workers, correctional agency staff, and policymakers. Its publications include the *Juvenile Justice Standards*, a twenty-four volume set of comprehensive juvenile justice standards; the report *More than Meets the Eye: Rethinking Assessment, Competency, and Sentencing for a Harsher Era of Juvenile Justice*; and the quarterly *Criminal Justice Magazine*.

American Civil Liberties Union (ACLU)
125 Broad St., New York, NY 10004
(212) 549-2900 • fax: (212) 869-9065
e-mail: aclu@aclu.org • website: www.aclu.org

The ACLU is a national organization that works to defend Americans' civil rights as guaranteed by the U.S. Constitution. It opposes curfew laws for juveniles and others and seeks to protect the public-assembly rights of gang members or people associated with gangs. Among the ACLU's numerous publications are the book *In Defense of American Liberties: A History of the ACLU*, the handbook *The Rights of Prisoners: A Comprehensive Guide to the Legal Rights of Prisoners Under Current Law*, and the briefing paper "Crime and Civil Liberties."

American Correctional Association (ACA)
4380 Forbes Blvd., Lanham, MD 20706
(800) 222-5646 • fax: (301) 918-1886
e-mail: jeffw@aca.org • website: www.corrections.com/aca

The ACA is composed of correctional administrators, prison wardens, superintendents, and other corrections professionals who want to improve correctional standards. The ACA studies the causes of crime and juvenile delinquency and reports regularly on juvenile justice issues in its monthly magazines *Corrections Today* and *Corrections Compendium*.

Center for the Study of Youth Policy
University of Pennsylvania School of Social Work
4200 Pine St., 2nd Floor, Philadelphia, PA 19104-4090
(215) 898-2229 • fax: (215) 573-2791
e-mail: yep@ssw.upenn.edu • website: www.kidspolicy.org
The center studies issues concerning juvenile justice and youth corrections. Although the center itself does not take positions regarding these issues, it publishes individuals' opinions in booklets, including *Home-Based Services for Serious and Violent Juvenile Offenders*, *Youth Violence: An Overview*, and *Mediation Involving Juveniles: Ethical Dilemmas and Policy Questions*.

Children of the Night
14530 Sylvan St., Van Nuys, CA 91411
(818) 908-4474 • crisis hotline: (800) 551-1300
fax: (818) 908-1468
e-mail: cotnll@aol.com • website: www.childrenofthenight.org
Children of the Night provides protection and support for street children, usually runaways, who are involved in pornography or prostitution. The organization places children with counselors and in drug programs and independent living situations, and it conducts a semiannual training laboratory for persons who wish to work with street children. Children of the Night publishes a variety of brochures.

Committee for Children
2203 Airport Way S., Suite 500, Seattle, WA 98134-2027
(206) 343-1223 • (800) 634-4449 • fax: (206) 343-1445
e-mail: info@cfchildren.org • website: www.cfchildren.org
The Committee for Children is an international organization that develops classroom curricula and videos as well as teacher, parent, and community training programs for the prevention of child abuse and youth violence. Second Step, the committee's violence prevention curriculum, teaches children social skills and provides training for parents and teachers to practice and reinforce these skills with children. The committee publishes the newsletter *Prevention Update* three times a year and developed the program *Sec-*

ond Step, which teaches children how to change behaviors and attitudes that contribute to violence.

Educational Fund to End Handgun Violence
Ceasefire Action Network
1000 16th St. NW, Suite 603, Washington, DC 20036
(202) 530-5888 • fax: (202) 544-7213
e-mail: edfund@aol.com • website: www.csgv.org

The fund examines and helps educate the public about handgun violence in the United States and how such violence affects children in particular. The fund participates in the development of educational materials and programs to help persuade teenagers not to carry guns, and it examines the impact of handguns on public health. Its publications include the booklet *Kids and Guns: A National Disgrace* and the quarterly newsletters *Assault Weapon and Accessories in America* and *Firearms Litigation Reporter.*

Gang Violence Bridging Project
Edmund G. "Pat" Brown Institute of Public Affairs
California State University
5151 State University Dr., Los Angeles, CA 90032-8261
(213) 343-3773 • fax: (213) 343-3774
e-mail: gsanche@calstatela.edu
website: www.gvbpla.freeservers.com

The project seeks to create communication among communities in the Los Angeles area. As an alternative to traditional suppressive measures such as incarceration, it advocates development of services and policies designed to prevent gang activity and to provide alternatives to gang membership. The project believes that the problem of gang violence must be addressed in the context of poverty, unemployment, and deteriorating schools and youth services. It publishes fact sheets on gang violence and related topics and a periodic newsletter, *PBI.*

The Heritage Foundation
214 Massachusetts Ave. NE, Washington, DC 20002
(202) 546-4400 • fax: (202) 546-8328
e-mail: info@heritage.org • website: www.heritage.org

The Heritage Foundation is a conservative public policy research institute. It advocates tougher sentences and the construction of more prisons as means to reduce crime. The foundation publishes the quarterly journal *Policy Review*, which occasionally contains articles addressing juvenile crime.

Milton S. Eisenhower Foundation
1660 L St. NW, Suite 200, Washington, DC 20036
(202) 429-0440 • fax: (202) 452-0169
e-mail: info@eisenhowerfoundation.org
website: www.eisenhowerfoundation.org

The foundation consists of individuals dedicated to reducing crime in inner-city neighborhoods through community programs. It believes that more federally funded programs such as Head Start and Job Corps would improve education and job opportunities for youths, thus reducing juvenile crime and violence. The foundation's publications include the report *To Establish Justice, to Insure Domestic Tranquility: A Thirty-Year Update of the National Commission on the Causes and Prevention of Violence* and the book *Youth Investment and Police Mentoring*.

National Center on Institutions and Alternatives (NCIA)
635 Slaters Ln., Suite G-100, Alexandria, VA 22314
(703) 684-0373 • fax: (703) 684-6037
e-mail: info@ncia.net • website: www.igc.org/ncia/home.html

The NCIA works to reduce the number of people institutionalized in prisons and mental hospitals. It favors the least restrictive forms of detention for juvenile offenders and opposes sentencing juveniles as adults and executing juvenile murderers. The NCIA publishes the report *Youth Homicide: Keeping Perspective on How Many Children Kill* and the article "Justice: Facts vs. Anger."

National Council of Juvenile and Family Court Judges
University of Nevada
1041 N. Virginia St., PO Box 8970, Reno, NV 89557
(775) 784-6012 • fax: (775) 784-6628
website: www.ncjfcj.unr.edu

The council is composed of juvenile and family court judges and other juvenile justice professionals. It seeks to improve juvenile and family court standards and practices. Its publications include the monthly *Juvenile and Family Law Digest* and the quarterly *Juvenile and Family Court Journal*.

National Council on Crime and Delinquency (NCCD)
685 Market St., Suite 620, San Francisco, CA 94105
(415) 896-6223 • fax: (415) 896-5109
e-mail: nccd@hooked.net • website: www.cascomm.com/users.nccd

The NCCD is composed of corrections specialists and others interested in the juvenile justice system and the prevention of crime and delinquency. It advocates community-based treatment programs rather than imprisonment for delinquent youths. It opposes placing minors in adult jails and executing those who commit capital offenses before the age of eighteen. The NCCD publishes the quarterlies *Crime and Delinquency* and *Journal of Research in Crime and Delinquency* as well as policy papers, including the "Juvenile Justice Policy Statement" and "Unlocking Juvenile Corrections: Evaluating the Massachusetts Department of Youth Services."

National Crime Prevention Council (NCPC)
1000 Connecticut Ave. NW, 8th Floor, Washington, DC 20006
(202) 466-6272 • fax: (202) 296-1356
e-mail: webmaster@ncpc.org • website: www.ncpc.org
The NCPC provides training and technical assistance to groups and individuals interested in crime prevention. It advocates job training and recreation programs as means to reduce youth crime and violence. The council, which sponsors the Take a Bite Out of Crime campaign, publishes the book *Changing Perspectives: Youth as Resources*, the booklet *Securing the Future for Safer Youth Communities*, and the newsletter *Catalyst*, which is published ten times a year.

National Juvenile Detention Association (NJDA)
Eastern Kentucky University
301 Perkins Building, 521 Lancaster Ave., Richmond, KY 40475-3102
(606) 622-6259 • fax: (606) 622-2333
e-mail: njda@njda.org • website: www.njda.org
The NJDA works to advance the science, processes, and art of juvenile detention through the overall improvement of the juvenile justice profession. The project's efforts include the delivery of quality products to juvenile justice and detention facilities, reviewing and establishing detention standards and practices, and stimulating the development of training programs for detention service officials. Its publications include the journal *Developing Comprehensive Systems for Troubled Youth* and the *Journal for Juvenile Justice and Detention Services*.

National School Safety Center (NSSC)
141 Duesenberg Dr., Suite 11, Westlake Village, CA 91362
(805) 373-9977 • fax: (805) 373-9277
e-mail: info@nssc1.org • website: www.nssc1.org
The NSSC is a research organization that studies school crime and violence, including hate crimes. The center believes that teacher training is an effective means of reducing these problems. Its publications include the book *Gangs in Schools: Breaking Up Is Hard to*

Do and the *School Safety Update* newsletter, which is published nine times a year.

Office of Juvenile Justice and Delinquency Prevention (OJJDP)

810 7th St. NW, Washington, DC 20531
(202) 307-5911 • fax: (202) 307-2093
e-mail: askjj@ojp.usdoj.gov • website: ojjdp.ncjrs.org

As the primary federal agency charged with monitoring and improving the juvenile justice system, the OJJDP develops and funds programs on juvenile justice. Among its goals are the prevention and control of illegal drug use and serious crime by juveniles. Through its Juvenile Justice Clearinghouse, the OJJDP distributes fact sheets and reports such as *Juvenile Offenders in Residential Placement* and *A Comprehensive Response to America's Youth Gang Problem.*

Youth Crime Watch of America

9300 S. Dadeland Blvd., Suite 100, Miami, FL 33156
(305) 670-2409 • fax: (305) 670-3805
e-mail: ycwa@ycwa.org • website: www.ycwa.org

Youth Crime Watch of America is dedicated to establishing Youth Crime Watch programs across the United States. It strives to give youths the tools and guidance necessary to actively reduce crime and drug use in their schools and communities. Its publications include *Talking to Youth About Crime Prevention*, the workbook *Community Based Youth Crime Watch Program Handbook*, and the motivational video *Put an End to School Violence Today.*

Youth Policy Institute (YPI)

1333 Green Court St. NW, Washington, DC 20005
(301) 585-0580 • fax: (202) 638-2325
e-mail: dixsling@aol.com

The YPI monitors federal policies concerning youth and family in order to provide information on these policies to organizations and individuals. The institute believes that much of youth violence results from violence on television and in movies. It also believes that schools and local communities should try to solve the problem of youth violence. The YPI publishes the monthly magazines *American Family and Youth Policy*, the triannual journal *Future Choices*, and the biweekly *Youth Record.*

Bibliography of Books

Robert Agnew — *Juvenile Delinquency: Causes and Control*. Los Angeles: Roxbury, 2000.

S. Beth Akin — *Voices from the Street: Young Former Gang Members Tell Their Stories*. Canada: Little, Brown, 1996.

James F. Anderson, Laronistine Dyson, and Jerald C. Burns — *Boot Camps: An Intermediate Sanction*. Lanham, MD: University Press of America, 2000.

Randy Blazak and Wayne S. Wooden — *Renegade Kids, Suburban Outlaws: From Youth Culture to Delinquency*. Florence, KY: Wadsworth, 2000.

Elaine Cassel and Douglas A. Bernstein — *Criminal Behavior*. Needham Heights, MD: Allyn and Bacon, 2000.

Gordon A. Crews and Reid H. Montgomery — *Chasing Shadows: Confronting Juvenile Violence in America*. Upper Saddle River, NJ: Prentice-Hall, 2001.

G. David Curry and Scott H. Decker — *Confronting Gangs: Crime and Community*. Los Angeles: Roxbury, 2001.

Joy G. Dryfoos — *Safe Passage: Making It Through Adolescence in a Risky Society*. New York: Oxford University Press, 2000.

Delbert S. Elliott, Beatrix A. Hamburg, and Kirk R. Williams — *Violence in American Schools*. Cambridge, MA: Cambridge University Press, 1998.

Mark S. Fleisher — *Dead End Kids: Gang Girls and the Boys They Know*. Madison, WI: University of Wisconsin Press, 1998.

Gustav Mark Gedatus — *Gangs and Violence (Perspectives on Violence)*. Santa Rosa, CA: Lifematters, 2000.

Denise C. Gottfredson — *Schools and Delinquency*. Cambridge, MA: Cambridge University Press, 2000.

John Hagan and Bill McCarthy — *Mean Streets: Youth Crime and Homelessness*. Cambridge, MA: Cambridge University Press, 1998.

J. David Hawkins — *Delinquency and Crime: Current Theories*. Cambridge, MA: Cambridge University Press, 1996.

Richard Hil and Anthony McMahon — *Families, Crime, and Juvenile Justice*. New York: Peter Lang, 2000.

Robert K. Jackson and Wesley D. McBride — *Street Gangs.* Incline Village, NE: Copperhouse, 1996.

Thomas A. Jacobs — *Teens on Trial: Twenty Teens Who Challenged the Law—and Changed Your Life.* Minneapolis: Free Spirit, 2000.

Dan B. Kates and Gary Kleck — *The Great American Gun Debate: Essays on Firearms and Violence.* San Francisco: Pacific Research Institute, 1997.

Richard Lawrence — *School Crime and Juvenile Justice.* New York: Oxford University Press, 1997.

Mike Males — *The Scapegoat Generation: America's War on Adolescents.* Monroe, ME: Common Courage Press, 1996.

Jody Miller — *One of the Guys: Girls, Gangs, and Gender.* New York: Oxford University Press, 2000.

Scott Minerbrook — *Divided to the Vein: A Journey into Race and Family.* New York: Harcourt Brace, 1996.

Mark H. Moore — *Youth Violence.* Chicago: University of Chicago Press, 1999.

Wilda Webber Morris — *Stop the Violence: Educating Ourselves to Protect Our Youth.* Valley Forge, PA: Judson Press, 2001.

Debra Niehoff — *The Biology of Violence.* New York: Free Press, 1999.

Howard Pinderhughes — *Race in the Hood: Conflict and Violence Among Urban Youth.* Minneapolis: University of Minnesota Press, 1997.

John Pitts — *The New Politics of Youth Crime: Discipline and Solidarity.* New York: St. Martin's Press, 2001.

Richard Rhodes — *Why They Kill: Discoveries of a Maverick Criminologist.* New York: Vintage Books, 1999.

Ronin Ro — *Gangsta: Merchandizing the Rhymes of Violence.* New York: St. Martin's Press, 1996.

Michael Rutter — *Antisocial Behavior by Young People.* Cambridge, MA: Cambridge University Press, 1998.

Simon I.I. Singer — *Recriminalizing Delinquency: Violent Juvenile Crime and Juvenile Justice Reform.* Cambridge, MA: Cambridge University Press, 1997.

Ved Varma — *Violence in Children and Adolescents.* Bristol, PA: Jessica Kingsley, 1997.

Joseph G. Weiss, Robert D. Crutchfield, and George S. Bridges	*Juvenile Delinquency: Readings*. Boston: Pine Forge Press, 2001.
Valerie Wiener	*Winning the War Against Youth Gangs*. Westport, CT: Greenwood Press, 1999.
Kenneth Wooden and Kathleen M. Heide	*Weeping in the Playtime of Others: America's Incarcerated Children*. Columbus: Ohio State University Press, 2000.
Frank E. Zimring	*American Youth Violence*. New York: Oxford University Press, 1998.

Index